ENCOUNTERING **JESUS** IN THE SCRIPTURES

EDITED BY Daniel J. Harrington, SJ,
AND Christopher R. Matthews

Paulist Press
New York / Mahwah, NJ

Cover image by Genotar/Shutterstock.com.

Cover and book design by Lynn Else

Library of Congress Cataloging-in-Publication Data

Encountering Jesus in the scriptures / edited by Daniel J. Harrington and Christopher R. Matthews.
    p. cm.
    ISBN 978-0-8091-4812-7 (alk. paper) — ISBN 978-1-58768-094-6 1. Bible. N.T.—Criticism, interpretation, etc. 2. Jesus Christ. I. Harrington, Daniel J. II. Matthews, Christopher R.
    BS2361.3.E53 2013
    232—dc23

2012039353

Published by Paulist Press
997 Macarthur Boulevard
Mahwah, New Jersey 07430

www.paulistpress.com

Printed and bound in the
United States of America

CONTENTS

Introduction 1

1. Jesus: What's Fact? What's Fiction? 5
   Daniel J. Harrington, SJ

2. Conceived by the Holy Spirit, Born of the
   Virgin Mary 13
   Barbara E. Bowe, RSCJ

3. Jesus and the Kingdom of God 20
   John R. Donahue, SJ

4. The Sermon on the Mount: What Is It? 24
   Daniel J. Harrington, SJ

5. The Miracles of Jesus 32
   Eugene Hensell, OSB

6. Up against Caesar: Jesus and Paul versus Empire 36
   John Dart

7. The Study of Women in the Early Church 46
   Carolyn Osiek, RSCJ

8. Misusing Jesus: How the Church Divorces Jesus
   from Judaism 53
   Amy-Jill Levine

CONTENTS

9. The Bible, the Jews, and the Passion..........................60
    Eugene J. Fisher

10. Telling the Terror of the Crucifixion 66
    Barbara E. Reid, OP

11. The Empty Tomb 73
    Gerald O'Collins, SJ

12. Apocryphal Gospels: Early Christian Piety and
    the Legendary Jesus......................................80
    Christopher R. Matthews

13. *Lectio Divina*: Bridging the Gap between God's
    Heart and Ours 89
    John Belmonte, SJ

14. Coming to Know Jesus through Contemplation
    of the Gospels 100
    William A. Barry, SJ

Further Reading on
Encountering Jesus in the Scriptures..............................105

Index..107

INTRODUCTION

Among the various significant issues addressed by the twenty-seven writings that make up the New Testament, two fundamental questions are, Who is Jesus? and Why is he important? The four Gospels look like biographies (at least in the ancient sense) and provide much information about Jesus's life, teachings, activities, and death. However, no one of them tells the whole story about Jesus. In fact, they all draw us back to the haunting question that Jesus posed to Peter and the other disciples, "But who do you say that I am?" (Mark 8:29).

In recent years that question has occasioned thousands of scholarly books and articles. This development from 1985 to the present is sometimes called the "Third Quest of the Historical Jesus." The First Quest took place from the late eighteenth to the early twentieth century and was brilliantly catalogued by Albert Schweitzer. The Second Quest refers to a brief period in the mid-1900s when some students of Rudolf Bultmann rejected his skepticism about Jesus and contended that we can know a good deal about Jesus's teachings. The first two quests were carried on almost entirely by liberal German Protestant historians and theologians. The Third Quest, by contrast, has been both international and confessionally diverse and has given special attention to the Jewishness of Jesus.

This volume seeks to make accessible some of the best modern scholarship to assist one in encountering Jesus in the scriptures. Its focus is wider than the historians' quest. These chapters try to explain not only who Jesus was in the first century but also what he might mean in the twenty-first century. Most of the contributors are Catholic scholars who have proved their ability to undertake serious technical research and to communicate the results of modern scholarship to nonspecialists.

The most authoritative Catholic document on biblical study is Vatican II's 1965 Constitution on Divine Revelation (*Dei verbum*). This document describes the scriptures as the word of God in human language and as the soul of theology and insists that the church's preaching be nourished and ruled by scripture. It encourages interpreters to be sensitive to the literary forms and cultural assumptions of the societies in which the biblical authors wrote. It recognizes that the four Gospels are the products of a fairly long and complex development from Jesus through the oral and written traditions of the early church to the Gospel writers (evangelists), while insisting that they tell us the honest truth about Jesus.

The editors of this volume have worked together for more than twenty-seven years on *New Testament Abstracts*, which is based at the Boston College School of Theology and Ministry. Our journal provides an objective report of current scholarship published in many different languages. In recent years, we have covered at least 2,100 articles and 800 books *per annum*. We believe that the chapters that follow present a sample of some positive and constructive research on Jesus today. The chapters first appeared in journals intended for the general public and so represent popularizations of more technical material. Then they (with one exception) appeared together in "tabloid newspaper" format in an issue of *C21 Resources*, a service of Boston College's Church in the 21st Century Center. We hope that in this new format, they may serve as a good introduction to one area of modern biblical scholarship and as a help for readers in answering Jesus's own question, "But who do you say that I am?"

Daniel J. Harrington, SJ, and Christopher R. Matthews

1

JESUS

WHAT'S FACT? WHAT'S FICTION?

Daniel J. Harrington, SJ

The question of Jesus's identity is central to us as Christians. Because Christianity is an incarnational faith—centered on Jesus, the Word of God who became flesh and dwelt among us—it is important to learn as much as we can about the Jesus of history. He lived in the land of Israel during what we now call the first century. The question of his identity still has great relevance for us in the early twenty-first century. Just consider the media attention received by Mel Gibson's *The Passion of the Christ* and Dan Brown's *The Da Vinci Code*. When Jesus asked his disciples, "Who do people say that I am?," he got several different answers: John the Baptist, Elijah, one of the prophets. Even when Peter identified Jesus correctly as the Messiah, Jesus felt the need to redefine messiahship in terms of his coming passion, death, and resurrection.

A DIFFICULT QUESTION

While important, the question about Jesus's identity is difficult to answer. It is hard to know the whole story about any person, even someone who has lived in our own time, let alone someone who lived 2,000 years ago.

The major sources about Jesus—the Gospels of Matthew, Mark, Luke, and John—were written in light of the authors' convictions about Jesus's resurrection and continued existence with the one whom he called Father. The claims that these authors made about Jesus (such as "Jesus is Lord") go beyond what is said about even the greatest human heroes.

Here I want to tell as best as I can the "honest truth" about what we can know about Jesus of Nazareth and thus provide a reasonably objective account against which the claims of Mel Gibson, Dan Brown, and others can be measured.

I write as a Roman Catholic priest, a Jesuit, and a professor of New Testament since 1971. In my academic research, I have taken special interest in the Dead Sea scrolls and other Jewish texts from the time of Jesus. As editor of *New Testament Abstracts*, I see all the books and articles published in the field.

MAJOR SOURCES

The four Gospels are the major sources for what we know about Jesus. Nevertheless, they do not allow us to write a full biography about him. Rather, the Gospel writers (evangelists) were primarily interested in Jesus's religious significance and his impact as a moral figure.

Mark's Gospel, written around AD 70, perhaps at Rome, tells the story of Jesus's public ministry in Galilee, his journey with his disciples to Jerusalem, and his short ministry there, as well as his passion, death, and resurrection. Mark gave special attention to Jesus as the suffering Messiah and to the mystery of the cross.

Between AD 85 and 90, Matthew and Luke independently produced their own revised and expanded versions of Mark's Gospel. They added a large amount of teaching material from other sources and traditions. Matthew emphasized the Jewishness of Jesus and his fulfillment of Israel's scriptures, the books of the Bible Christians commonly call the Old Testament. Luke stressed Jesus's significance not only for Israel but also for the other peoples of the world. Because the first three Gospels offer a common outline and vision of Jesus, they are often called the "Synoptic" Gospels, which means "viewed with one eye or lens."

While John's Gospel has much in common with the Synoptic Gospels and contains many pieces of solid historical information, it spreads the public ministry of Jesus over three years instead of one, introduces different characters, and focuses more on Jesus as the revealer and revelation of God than on the kingdom.

These four Gospels became part of the church's list of approved books (canon) because of their wide use, orthodox theological content, and association with the apostles.

OTHER SOURCES

The noncanonical Gospels attributed to Thomas, Peter, Mary Magdalene, Philip, and others did not become part of the church's New Testament canon. This was due in part to their lack of wide usage, sometimes unorthodox theological content, and relatively late dates of composition.

These sources now often serve as the basis for works like *The Da Vinci Code* and other, often sensationalist interpretations of early Christianity—some even by well-known scholars. They may contain some early authentic traditions, though it is often difficult to isolate these from their less credible content. Likewise, while there are stray sayings attributed to Jesus in other early Christian writings, it is almost impossible to prove they originated with Jesus.

The only substantial ancient description of Jesus apart from Christian sources appears in *Jewish Antiquities* by Flavius Josephus, a Jewish historian in the late first century AD. But the explicit statements about Jesus's identity as the Messiah and about his resurrection suggest that Christian scribes may have inserted their own convictions about Jesus into Josephus's work.

Josephus wrote, "About this time arose Jesus, a wise man, if indeed it be lawful to call him a man. For he was a doer of wonderful deeds, and a teacher of men who . . . drew to himself many, both of the Jews and the Gentiles. He was the Christ" (18:63–64, Loeb Classical Library translation).

GOSPEL DEVELOPMENT

The early Christians were more concerned with experiencing the risen Jesus and the Holy Spirit than with writing books about Jesus. Jesus died around AD 30, and the first complete Gospel (Mark's) appeared forty years later. In those intervening decades there was a lively process in which traditions from and about Jesus, whether in oral or written form, were handed on among Christians. These traditions were often shaped and reshaped in response to the pastoral needs of the communities.

Understanding the process by which the Gospels were formed requires keeping three realities in mind: the focus of the evangelist, the development of the early church, and who Jesus was. The Gospel writers composed the final forms of their works with an eye toward their significance for particular communities. The gathered materials had been formulated and adapted in various settings over forty or more years. And, of course, they all sought to tell us the "honest truth" about Jesus, as best they could.

GETTING BACK TO JESUS

Are there ways of going behind the Gospel texts and the traditions of the early church and getting back to Jesus himself? Biblical scholars have developed several tools to isolate material in the Gospels that most likely goes back to Jesus. If a teaching is unlike anything in Jewish and early Christian traditions, then it probably can be assigned directly to Jesus. An example would be Jesus's absolute prohibition of taking oaths: "Do not swear at all" (Matt 5:34).

Other such criteria include: when a tradition appears in several different sources (Last Supper); local Palestinian coloring (Aramaic words, farming methods); embarrassment at what might reflect badly on Jesus (his reception of John's "baptism of repentance for the forgiveness of sins"); what led to Jesus's death (the "cleansing" of the Temple); and coherence (what fits with what can be established by other criteria).

These historical methods do not tell us everything we would like to know about Jesus. Nor do they necessarily establish what was most important about him. But they do tell us something.

JESUS'S MINISTRY

Study of the Gospels and application of these historical criteria make it possible to develop at least an outline of Jesus's public career. Having been raised in Nazareth in Galilee, Jesus accepted baptism from John and may have been a member of John's movement.

When Jesus went out on his own to continue and

adapt John's mission, he gathered disciples near the Sea of Galilee at Capernaum, including some of John's followers. He spent much of his public life preaching about the kingdom of God and how to prepare for it. He also healed the sick as a sign of the presence of God's kingdom.

Before Passover in the spring of AD 30, Jesus and his followers made a long journey to Jerusalem. There he continued his ministry of teaching and healing, but ran into intense opposition from some other Jews and from the Roman authorities. Under the Roman prefect, Pontius Pilate, Jesus was executed by crucifixion as a rebel and a religious troublemaker. And he was said to have appeared alive again to some of his followers.

Careful study of the Gospels also allows us to reconstruct the major themes in Jesus's teaching. At the center was the reign or kingdom of God in both its present and future dimensions. Jesus's relationship to God was so close that he dared to address God as Father and invited others to do the same. He proclaimed the possibility of the forgiveness of sins and of reconciliation with God.

Jesus challenged his followers to love their enemies and told them how to act in anticipation of the coming kingdom of God. He showed special concern for marginal persons— the poor, the lame, "sinners and tax collectors," prostitutes, and so on—and manifested a free attitude toward the traditions associated with the Jewish Law and the Jerusalem Temple. Most of these themes appear in the Lord's Prayer that Jesus taught to his disciples.

HISTORICAL QUEST

The Jesus whom modern historians can recover and investigate by using the tools of historical research is sometimes called the "historical Jesus." A more accurate term would be the "historian's Jesus." This Jesus is not the whole person of Jesus, nor is he the traditional object of Christian faith. The one whom Christians worship is not only the earthly Jesus but also—and especially—the risen Jesus who will come again in glory. Christians believe that there is a close continuity between the earthly Jesus and the Christ of faith and that the two cannot be totally separated.

The quest for the historical Jesus, however, refers to the project of separating the earthly Jesus from the Christ of faith. It began among liberal German Protestants in the late eighteenth century in an effort to peel away the wrappings given to Jesus in church tradition and to recover the simple figure of the "real" Jesus. Many of the early seekers discarded the miracles of Jesus and rejected his virginal conception and resurrection as "unhistorical." One positive development was the recognition of the kingdom of God as the focus of Jesus's teaching and its roots in Jewish hopes about God's future actions on behalf of his people (sometimes called eschatology or apocalyptic writing).

The quest in the twentieth century focused on the parables of Jesus as a way of recovering the "voice" of Jesus about the kingdom, developing criteria for identifying material from Jesus, and situating Jesus within Judaism. Recent presentations of Jesus have depicted him as a prophet sent to speak of the end times, a wisdom teacher, a philosopher, and a poet skilled in his use of parables and images.

MEANING FOR TODAY

While charged with frustration, the quest for the historical Jesus has been a fascinating and even irresistible topic. It reminds us that there is no uninterpreted Jesus and that we are dependent on sources that historians find challenging.

For people of faith, the witness of the Gospels is more important than the historian's Jesus. Nevertheless, historical methods can help us to see the basic reliability of the tradition about Jesus and to encounter Jesus as the strong personality behind the Gospels and the traditions and truths contained in them.

NOTES

This chapter is reprinted with permission from *St. Anthony Messenger* 114, no. 1 (2006): 13–16.

2

CONCEIVED BY THE HOLY SPIRIT, BORN OF THE VIRGIN MARY

Barbara E. Bowe, RSCJ

The birth of every human being is in some real sense a miraculous event. Biologically, the joining of egg and sperm, the combination of X and Y chromosomes, the slow process of development in the mother's womb, and finally the mystery of birth itself produces awe and wonder in even the most hardened and stoic person. The gift of new life in the birth of a child draws all of us who witness it close to God. No wonder then that the psalmist turns to this image to speak about the mystery of human life and God's creative shaping of the human person:

> You have formed my inmost being;
> you knit me in my mother's womb.
> I praise you, so wonderfully you made me;
> wonderful are your works.   (Ps 139:13–14)

But how much more astonishing is the birth of the Son of God!

"WE BELIEVE"

By the creedal affirmation that Jesus was "conceived by the Holy Spirit, born of the virgin Mary," we profess our belief in the extraordinary miracle of the birth of the Son of God. Two truths are contained here. The first phrase attests that Jesus's birth was "by the impulse of the Spirit of the Holy," as Sr. Joan Chittister, OSB, has said so well.[1] It was not an ordinary conception like yours and mine. It was brought about by the mysterious power of God's Spirit.

The second phrase claims that Jesus was born of Mary; that is, he came into the human world the way every one of us came into it—from the body of a woman. And he received from his mother the fullness of humanity. He was indeed truly God and truly a human being. These affirmations, however, stand in tension—humanity and divinity coalesce in the birth of Jesus. However, these creedal statements are not so much about the biology of Jesus's conception and birth but about the fact of his birth coming about through the awesome cooperation of God and the woman, Mary. They do not tell us how this happened; they only affirm that it happened. These creedal affirmations rely on and are grounded in the witness of the faith experience of the earliest Christians and in the stories of Jesus contained in our scriptures.

ONE JESUS, FOUR GOSPEL STORIES

The earliest written witness to the life, words, and deeds of Jesus is, in fact, not any one of the four Gospels but the letters of the apostle Paul. When you think about it, however, if we only had the letters of Paul, how much would we know about Jesus? The answer is, precious little. Paul's central fascination and claim about Jesus is that his death

and resurrection, what we call the paschal mystery, has ush-
ered in a new age and opened up the promise of salvation to
Jew and Gentile alike. Though he surely must have known
them, he shows no interest in telling the details of the stories of Jesus's life and public ministry, and says nothing specific about Jesus's entry into our world. One thing that Paul
does affirm about Jesus is the fact of his being "born of a
woman, born under the law" (Gal 4:4). For Paul, the human
birth of Jesus of Nazareth was an obvious fact. Therefore,
Paul emphasized that Jesus shared with every one of us the
condition of being truly human by virtue of our common
human birth "of a woman."

The earliest of our four Gospels—the Gospel of Mark
—also begins its story of Jesus not with the story of the circumstances of his birth, but with the opening of Jesus's adult
public ministry in Galilee. Mark, like Paul, holds a firm conviction of Jesus's humanness and takes every opportunity in
the Gospel to call the readers' attention to Jesus's human
emotions, to his human family and relatives, and to his ago-
nizing experience of human death. Yet Mark, like Paul, is
convinced that God raised Jesus from the dead and that he
is truly, as the centurion acclaimed, "the Son of God" (Mark
15:39). Mark seems to suggest that this sonship was the
result of his death and resurrection when he was taken up
to God as true son, although already at his baptism God
proclaimed Jesus as his beloved son (1:11).

THE INFANCY NARRATIVES OF
MATTHEW AND LUKE

But as the Christian movement matured during the
first century, its understanding of Jesus's identity deepened
and increased. We find therefore that the Gospels of
Matthew and Luke preserve stories (albeit very different

stories) about the extraordinary circumstances of Jesus's conception and birth. It is important to recognize that the infancy narratives in these two Gospels are primarily theologically motivated and they do not pretend to describe with medical precision and scientific accuracy (nor could they) the exact biology of Jesus's birth. Our creedal faith points toward a mystery that cannot be fully explained or reduced to medical analysis.

For Matthew's Gospel, the essential affirmations about Jesus are his Davidic descent, accomplished through Joseph's adoption of the child, and his birth through the Holy Spirit: "Now this is how the birth of Jesus Christ came about. When his mother Mary was betrothed to Joseph, but before they lived together, she was found with child through the Holy Spirit" (Matt 1:18). A few verses later Matthew records the angel's message to Joseph that explains further how this extraordinary birth will happen: "Joseph, son of David, do not be afraid to take Mary as your wife into your home. For it is through the Holy Spirit that this child has been conceived in her" (Matt 1:20). The essential theological point that Matthew affirms is the conviction that Jesus did not slowly develop a oneness with God during his lifetime, or become one with God at his death, resurrection, and ascension to God, but that from the very moment of his conception Jesus was one with God through the power of the Holy Spirit. Matthew stresses Mary's virginity to affirm this truth about Jesus: that his conception happened through the power of the Spirit. Four centuries later, after continued discussion and reflection, the great church council of Chalcedon (AD 451) would provide a more precise philosophical grounding for this claim about Jesus's oneness with God. But for Matthew, it was enough to say simply that it was so.

Luke's infancy story makes similar claims, although his account is told entirely through the perspective of Mary's experience and not through Joseph's as in Matthew. With vivid and dramatic detail, Luke describes the appearance of the angel to Mary. The angel's words are perhaps the best-known part of our Christmas story celebrated each year: "Do not be afraid, Mary, for you have found favor with God. Behold, you will conceive in your womb and bear a son, and you shall name him Jesus" (Luke 1:30–31). Mary at first questions the message: "How can this be?" (Luke 1:34). She is no passive agent in this momentous event. She is a discerning collaborator with God's plans. So the angel explains: "The Holy Spirit will come upon you, and the power of the Most High will overshadow you. Therefore the child to be born will be called holy, the Son of God" (Luke 1:35). Like Matthew, Luke does not give us a biological or scientific explanation. He speaks in theological terms. The Spirit of God, that same Spirit that had hovered over the chaos waters at the beginning of time (Gen 1:2) and had inspired the prophets of old (for example, Isa 61:1–3) now will rest on this woman of Nazareth. Mary's *fiat*, "yes," signals her full cooperation with God in the mystery of the child's birth—a truly human birth, and at the same time a birth made possible by God's Holy Spirit.

"THE WORD BECAME FLESH"

The latest of the Gospels, the Gospel of John, does not take up and expand the birth and infancy narratives of Matthew and Luke. The author surely knows of the central role of Jesus's mother and she indeed is present at the "birth" of his ministry when the water became wine at Cana (John 2:2–5). She is there too at the end, as the symbolic presence of his new family at the close of his human life (John 19:25–27). John identifies Jesus also as a "son of Joseph" (John 1:45; 6:42), claiming his human family ties. But the Fourth Gospel says nothing at all of Jesus's human birth. Instead the Gospel of John opens with a poetic affirmation of the preexistence of the Logos, the Word of God, who "became flesh and made his dwelling among us" (John 1:14). John's story of Jesus begins not with his human birth but with his life as Logos-with-God before all time. Like Matthew and Luke, however, John's claim about Jesus's preexistent life and his "becoming flesh" is not about the biology of his birth, but about the certainty that here we have encountered a person in whom the human and divine have mingled. All four evangelists prepare the way for the creedal confession that "he was conceived by the Holy Spirit and born of the virgin Mary" by their insistence that in Jesus people encountered a man who was like them in his humanness, but at the same time a man who was suffused with the very Spirit and presence of God.

WHAT DO "WE BELIEVE"?

The church's faith grew and deepened in the early centuries that led finally to the great church councils of Nicea (AD 325) and Chalcedon (AD 451), when the intuitions and hunches of the New Testament writers found formal expression and philosophical precision in the creeds. What do we really believe by our affirmations of Jesus's conception by the Holy Spirit and birth from the body of Mary of Nazareth? Our faith is a testimony to the power of the Spirit working through the very ordinariness of our humanity. Jesus, the holy one of God, has become one with us. This claim of our faith means that our humanness is holy, that Jesus shared all that we are. In his birth from Mary he shows us that our flesh is not evil, that our bodiliness is good and leads us to God. By confessing that Jesus's birth happened through the mysterious power of the divine Spirit, we acknowledge at the same time that he is one with God, that his life offers us a way to God. Our faith tells us that Jesus's life, death, and resurrection has won for us salvation and the possibility of fullness of life with God forever.

This article of our creed, finally, says something very significant about our salvation. Luke Johnson puts it this way: "If, as Christians believe, the salvation brought by Jesus Christ fundamentally altered the structures of human existence itself, the moments of conception and birth are deservedly singled out by the creed, for the full sharing of the human condition by God's Son is fundamental (Heb 2:14–18)."[2] So we repeat our age-old confession of faith that he "was conceived by the Holy Spirit, born of the virgin Mary." And to that we say "Amen."

NOTES

This chapter is reprinted with permission from *The Bible Today* 43 (2005): 309–13.

1. Joan Chittister, *In Search of Belief* (Liguori, MO: Liguori Publications, 1999).

2. Luke T. Johnson, *The Creed: What Christians Believe and Why It Matters* (New York: Doubleday, 2003), 160.

3

JESUS AND THE KINGDOM OF GOD

John R. Donahue, SJ

The kingdom of God assumes a central place in contemporary New Testament scholarship. A wide spectrum of New Testament scholars of all denominations significantly agrees that the central theme of the public proclamation of Jesus was the arrival of God's powerful reign. Beyond this consensus is a virtual storm of scholarly discussion and debate. The kingdom is a major topic in three recent scholarly tomes: *Jesus: A Marginal Jew*, vol. 2, by John P. Meier;[1] *Jesus and the Victory of God*, by N. T. Wright;[2] and *Jesus Remembered*, by James D. G. Dunn.[3] The Greek term itself, *basileia tou theou* (literally, "kingdom of God"), expresses the power of God active in the ministry of Jesus, but it also implies a spatial or local dimension, as in "United Kingdom." The expression is a tensive symbol, evoking a host of associations rather than a single referent. The proclamation has a clear eschatological dimension—the final and definitive rule of God is at hand.

A host of problems accompany interpretation of this proclamation. There are three principal groups of sayings. The first stresses the presence of the kingdom; the second, its future coming; the third, its demands on people who wish to accept or enter it. A seemingly endless debate centers on which sayings are closest to the actual statements of Jesus (his *ipsissima vox*). Advocates of the presence of the kingdom interpret Jesus primarily as a prophet of reform (John Dominic Crossan), while the future sayings form the basis of interpreting Jesus as an apocalyptic preacher (Albert Schweitzer). Current exegesis leans toward some version of the thesis of Joachim Jeremias, that Jesus proclaims God's reign as already at work in his ministry, while anticipating its fullest realization in the future.

Evidence for both positions is ample. Jesus inaugurates his public ministry by proclaiming that the kingdom of God is at hand and summoning people to reform and renewal (*metanoia*, Mark 1:14–15). Jesus also proclaims that the kingdom is "among you" (Luke 17:21), not "within you," a translation that spawns many inaccurate appropriations. His mighty works of healing, confrontation with demons, and his power over nature are the signs of God's power now at work in his life and teaching. The kingdom is "of God," both as gift and challenge; despite common parlance, nowhere does the New Testament speak of "building the kingdom of God." For his part, Jesus speaks often of the kingdom in parables drawn from the ordinary lives of his hearers. Human experience is the path toward the transcendent.

Future expectation is also strong. Disciples are to pray that the kingdom will come, just as they pray for God's will to be done on earth as in heaven (Matt 6:10). Other sayings of Jesus reflect Jewish apocalyptic thought, with its emphasis on the end of the world, when the exalted Son of Man will reign as king to judge evildoers and restore justice to the elect (the sheep and the goats, Matt 25:31–46). According to Paul, eschatological fulfillment of the reign of God will come when at the end time the risen Jesus will hand over his kingdom to "his God and Father" (1 Cor 15:24).

The radical challenge of the kingdom is crystallized in a series of sayings on conditions for "entering" the kingdom. Rather than scandalize a child or commit other sins, one should be willing to enter the kingdom of God blind (Mark 9:47). Those who wish to enter the kingdom should be powerless like children (Matt 19:14); riches provide an overwhelming obstacle to entering (Matt 19:23–25). Disciples who seek the prestige of sitting at the right hand of Jesus in the kingdom are urged instead to become servants and slaves (Matt 20:21–28).

The powerful reign of God is not otherworldly, but embodied in history. Its arrival brings special hope to the poor, the suffering, and the marginal. When Jesus calls the poor happy because "the kingdom of God is yours" (Luke 6:20), he is declaring that God's reign is on their behalf. After the rich young man fails to heed Jesus's call to give his wealth to the poor, Jesus comments to his disciples about the young man's reluctance, "How hard it is for the rich to enter the kingdom of God" (Mark 10:23).

Jesus's personal consciousness of the reign of God constitutes an enduring problem. Though, apart from John 18, Jesus never refers to "his kingdom" and does not accept the title "king," he has a unique relationship to God's reign. For decades, scholars have called attention to Origen's description of Jesus as *autobasileia* (literally, "himself the kingdom"). Recent magisterial statements have frequently appealed to this text. While reflecting on Matthew 18:23–35, Origen in his commentary on Matthew says that "king" refers to the Son of God. He goes on to ask: Since Jesus is "wisdom itself" (*autosophia*), "justice itself" (*autodikaiosyne*), and "truth itself" (*autoasphaleia*), is he not also *autobasileia* "the kingdom itself"?

Origen prefers the spiritual sense over the literal, and his commentary is allegorical and christological. The phrase "the kingdom itself," therefore, is a theological expression on the trajectory that leads to the councils of Ephesus and Chalcedon. It is an interpretation, rather than a description of the historical Jesus.

NOTES

This chapter is reprinted with permission from *America* 197, no. 7 (2007): 16–17.

1. (New York: Doubleday, 1994); reviewed in *America*, April 8, 1995.

2. (Minneapolis: Fortress, 1996); reviewed in *America*, March 8, 1997.

3. (Grand Rapids: Eerdmans, 2003); reviewed in *America*, December 3, 2003.

4

THE SERMON ON THE MOUNT

WHAT IS IT?

Daniel J. Harrington, SJ

The Sermon on the Mount in Matthew 5—7 is arguably the best-known part of the Bible. If people today know any Bible passages at all, they probably know the beatitudes (Matt 5:3–12), the Lord's Prayer (6:9–13), the "lilies of the field" (6:28–30), and the Golden Rule (7:12). All these are from the Sermon on the Mount. Great Christian (Martin Luther King) and non-Christian (Gandhi) leaders of the twentieth century appealed to its principles in their campaigns for justice and freedom. Its influence on Christian ethics and moral theology has been enormous. The Sermon on the Mount is widely admired and loved, and its importance is beyond measure.

But what is it? This chapter answers that question first descriptively by looking at the sermon's origin, context, and content. Then it takes up the more difficult questions of genre and theological significance. Although it is relatively easy to describe the sermon, it is much more difficult to say how it should be understood and used as a guide to Christian life.

ORIGIN, CONTEXT, AND CONTENT

The Sermon on the Mount was composed by Matthew the evangelist (though Hans Dieter Betz, who has written a major commentary on the sermon, claims that it existed as a unit even before the Gospel's composition). Matthew wrote in the late first century AD for a largely Jewish Christian community, possibly at Antioch in Syria. His work was a revised and expanded version of Mark's Gospel in which he integrated material from the Sayings Source "Q" and from a special tradition (or traditions) found only in Matthew's Gospel and commonly referred to as "M." Matthew sought to give a larger sample of Jesus's teaching than was in Mark and to present Jesus as the authoritative representative and interpreter of the Jewish tradition in the crisis facing all Jews after the destruction of the Jerusalem Temple in AD 70.

In composing the Sermon on the Mount, Matthew used the block of Jesus's teaching in Q that appears in Luke as the Sermon on the Plain (Luke 6:20–49). He supplemented this foundational piece with other sayings that either are concerned with Jewish life or breathe the air of Jewish Wisdom literature. Since Matthew assembled and edited these traditions, it is fair to call the composition Matthew's Sermon on the Mount.

Nevertheless, Matthew lets us hear the voice of Jesus, even though it is unlikely that Jesus delivered this sermon word for word. Jesus taught in Aramaic, and Matthew wrote in Greek on the basis of Greek sources. Moreover, the content of the sermon is so rich that no audience could absorb it at one hearing. And yet the Sermon on the Mount contains teachings that modern scholars attribute with confidence to the historical Jesus: the beatitudes, the prohibitions of divorce and oaths, love of enemies, the Lord's Prayer, and so on. In that sense, Matthew's Sermon on the Mount allows us to hear Jesus's voice.

The Sermon on the Mount is the first of five great speeches by Jesus in Matthew's Gospel. The other discourses deal with discipleship (Matt 10), the kingdom of heaven (13), community life (18), and preparation for the full coming of the kingdom (24—25). Placed first in the series, the Sermon on the Mount (5—7) serves as a summary or compendium of Jesus's most important and distinctive teachings.

The sermon appears in the context of Matthew's narrative of Jesus's birth and his emergence from the circle of John the Baptist (1:1—4:16). As readers we know that Jesus is not only the son of Abraham and son of David but also the Son of God. We know that Jesus burst on the public scene proclaiming the coming kingdom of heaven (4:17) and summoning disciples (4:18–22). The audience for the sermon includes not only his small circle of disciples but also the crowds gathered from all the surrounding regions (see 4:24—5:2; 7:28–29).

THE SERMON AND JESUS

The sermon is followed in Matthew 8—9 by a series of miracle stories in which Jesus appears as a healer, exorcist, and miracle worker. The one who is powerful in word (as shown in the Sermon on the Mount) is also powerful in deed (as shown in his mighty acts). Then in the second great discourse (Matt 10), Jesus invites his disciples to do what he does—to teach, to proclaim the kingdom of God, and to heal the sick (see 4:23; 9:35; and 10:1, 7–8). Thus, the sermon is part of the story of Jesus, not a self-standing ethical treatise.

Matthew's Sermon on the Mount consists of five major sections. The introductory part (5:3–16) presents in 5:3–12 the beatitudes ("Blessed are the poor in spirit..."), which set forth the personal characteristics, values, attitudes, and actions that will be rewarded in the fullness of God's kingdom and are therefore to be cultivated in the present. The importance of those who follow Jesus's teaching and the service that they perform for the world is expressed with the help of three images in 5:13–16: the salt of the earth, the light of the world, and the city built on a hill.

The second part (5:17–48) concerns Jesus and the Jewish Law. The fundamental assertions in 5:17–20 are that Jesus came "not to abolish but to fulfill" the Law and the Prophets and that his approach is superior to that of the scribes and Pharisees. That Jesus offers deepening and an intensification rather than abolition is then illustrated by the six "antitheses" about murder and anger (5:21–26), adultery and lust (5:27–30), marriage and divorce (5:31–32), oaths (5:33–37), retaliation and nonviolence (5:38–42), and love of enemies (5:43–48).

The third part (6:1–18) deals with acts of piety: almsgiving (6:2–4), prayer (6:5–6), and fasting (6:16–18). The wrong way to perform acts of piety is to make a public spectacle in the hope of getting a good reputation for holiness. The right way is to seek to serve and please God alone. Also included are teachings about brevity in prayer (6:7–8), how to pray—the Lord's Prayer (6:9–13), and forgiveness (6:14–15).

The fourth part (6:19—7:12) provides wise advice about various topics: treasures (6:19–21), eyes (6:22–23), masters (6:24), anxiety (6:25–34), judgments (7:1–5), dogs and pigs (7:6), prayer (7:7–11), and the Golden Rule (7:12).

The concluding exhortation (7:13–27) uses short parables about gates and ways (7:13–14), trees and fruits (7:15–20), and houses and foundations (7:24–27) to highlight the challenges involved in practicing Jesus's teachings and the need for integrity and spiritual depth. It is not enough to know Jesus's teachings and to call him "Lord" (7:21–23). One must also do what he says. His wisdom is practical rather than purely speculative.

GENRE AND THEOLOGICAL SIGNIFICANCE

The Sermon on the Mount is a summary of Jesus's wise teachings. Some scholars compare it to the epitomes or compendia that were used in antiquity to summarize the doctrines of philosophers. However, given Jesus's (and Matthew's) roots in Judaism and the Jewish character of his teachings, a better analogy can be found among the wisdom instructions in Proverbs, Ecclesiastes, Sirach, and the Wisdom of Solomon.

In a wisdom instruction, the sage addresses those in search of wisdom. The sage uses various literary forms: beatitudes, proverbs, and commands and prohibitions often accompanied by reasons ("for…"), general principles, parables, and so on. While there is often an architecture or external framework in wisdom instructions, there is no extended argument or logical development of an idea. Instead the sage moves rapidly from topic to topic, sometimes only on the basis of key words or catchwords. The content embraces general principles, attitudes, and actions. All these features appear in Matthew 5—7, and to that extent, it is fair to call the Sermon on the Mount a wisdom instruction.

What is the Sermon on the Mount? To describe the origin, context, content, and literary genre of this text still does not fully answer the question. In fact, it generates another set of questions. How are we to understand it? What significance does it have for us? What are we to do with it?

It is probably easier to say what the Sermon on the

Mount is not than what it is. It is not an elitist or perfectionist ethics, intended only for a few individuals or a small group. Rather, it addresses not only Jesus's inner circle but also the crowds. It is not an impossible ethics (as Martin Luther proposed), designed to make us recognize our sinfulness and our need for God's grace. Rather, it is presented as something that people can put into practice (see 7:13–27). And it is not an interim ethics (at least in the narrow sense suggested by Albert Schweitzer) put forward by Jesus who mistakenly imagined that God's kingdom would come in a very short time. Matthew wrote some sixty years after Jesus's death.

Neither is the Sermon on the Mount a law code. Instead, it freely mixes general principles such as love of enemies (5:43–48) and the Golden Rule (7:12) with parables, exhortations, examples, declarations, and so on. Nor is it the new Torah. Instead, it presents Jesus as the authoritative interpreter of the Law of Moses and puts forward as his basic principle "not to abolish but to fulfill" (5:17).

But what is it? The Sermon on the Mount presents the wisdom of Jesus. In his initial wisdom instruction according to Matthew, Jesus lays out his teachings on true happiness, the interpretation of the Law and the Prophets, the service of God, and wise attitudes and actions in various spheres of human life. He concludes with a reminder about the practical nature of his wisdom. In form and content, Matthew 5—7 is a Jewish wisdom instruction.

CHRISTIAN CHARACTER AND CONDUCT

What significance does the Sermon on the Mount have for us? What do we do with it? The sermon is best understood today as part of an ethics of Christian character or Christian virtue ethics. The horizon and goal is the kingdom of God. The sermon tells how to prepare to enjoy its fullness and to act appropriately in the present. The search for "perfection" takes God as its model and criterion: "Be perfect, therefore, as your heavenly Father is perfect" (5:48). Its ethical teachings appear as part of a narrative in which Jesus is not only the master teacher but also the best example of his own teaching.

Being a student in Jesus's wisdom school involves formation in character and commitment to certain ways of acting. Rather than providing a complete code of conduct, the Sermon on the Mount shapes Christians to discern wisely and to act correctly. The sermon presupposes life in community and its positive impact for the common good as the salt of the earth, the light of the world, and the city on a hill.

The sermon makes no sharp distinction between law and love. Rather, they work together. The body of the sermon begins with Jesus's claim that he came "not to abolish but to fulfill" the Law and the Prophets (5:17). It ends with the Golden Rule: "In everything, do to others as you would have them do to you; for this is the Law and the Prophets" (7:12).

Various motives are offered for why one should act wisely and do good: entering the kingdom of heaven, imitating the example of God, going to the root of a divine commandment, behaving in a wise and appropriate manner, avoiding punishment in the present or in the world to come, and so on. There is no single motive to the exclusion of all others.

Another way to approach the present significance of the Sermon on the Mount is to compare it with the American Declaration of Independence and the Bill of Rights. These foundational documents express the vision of the Founding Fathers and the commonly accepted principles on which the United States is built. They contain the basic attitudes, ideals, and stances that serve as norms for legislation and behavior. They also set limits or parameters. And yet these documents, since they are well over two hundred years old, reflect a very different social and historical situation from our own. And they do not address issues that either were not regarded as imperative or practical in the late eighteenth century (abolition of slavery, women's suffrage, and so on) or that have been raised by modern technology (cloning, surrogate motherhood, weapons of mass destruction, and so on), while devoting great energy to matters that we now happily regard as resolved (freedom of assembly, of the press, of religion, and so on). Like the Sermon on the Mount, these documents need continuing interpretation, adaptation, and application. And yet they remain foundational, normative, and meaningful.

CONCLUSION

What is the Sermon on the Mount? It is Matthew's composition on the basis of earlier sources that allows us to hear the voice of Jesus the wise teacher. The first of the five great discourses in Matthew's narrative of Jesus, it deals with true happiness, the proper interpretation of the Law and the Prophets, genuine piety, wise attitudes and behavior in everyday life, and the need to translate wisdom into action. As a Jewish wisdom instruction, it expresses the wisdom of Jesus. Today it is best taken as proposing an ethics of Christian character or a Christian virtue ethics. It is foundational for Christian life, but it always requires interpretation, adaptation, and application.

NOTES

This chapter is reprinted with permission from *The Bible Today* 36 (1998): 280–86.

5

THE MIRACLES OF JESUS

Eugene Hensell, OSB

All four Gospels attest that Jesus worked miracles. In the Gospel of Mark, the first nine chapters are structured around the miracles of Jesus. Obviously, these actions of Jesus were very important to the evangelists and to the sources from which they received their material. Quite often, the stories of Jesus that people today find themselves most drawn to come from his miracles. There can be no doubt that miracles play a very significant role in the life and ministry of Jesus as portrayed in the Gospels. What is not so clear, however, is how these actions of Jesus are to be understood. What are they and what do they mean?

Traditionally the interpretation of miracles has been undertaken from one of two extremes. The first extreme comes from the literalists. This approach claims that the miracles describe actions that Jesus literally did in the exact manner the biblical text narrates them. They are literal, factual events that must be taken at face value. The second extreme comes from the rationalists. This approach stems from an understanding of truth being based solely on reason. Here it is said that the miracles of Jesus cannot be understood at face value because as such they are unreasonable. Instead, the interpreter must look at them through the eyes of reason and show how they can be explained through natural reasonable causes. Whatever cannot be explained in this way must be dismissed as false and untenable. The problem with both of these approaches is that they attempt to answer the wrong question. That wrong question is, What really happened?

There is no way that we can ever reconstruct historically what really happened when Jesus did a miracle. That was never the intent of the Gospel writers. Some like to think that, if one could prove that Jesus really did miracles, then that would also prove that he was God. Nothing could be further from the truth. At the time of Jesus, many holy men and women were believed to be able to do miracles. While this was considered to be a manifestation of holiness, it was never understood to manifest divinity. What was at stake in a miracle was not divinity but power.

Miracle workers were special people who were understood to have the ability to mediate power, both for good and for evil. The ancients never raised the question whether or not a miracle worker really could perform miracles. The question raised was what kind of power is behind this miracle. Miracles were based on what was considered ordinary or beyond human capacity. Of course, how one defines "ordinary" is influenced very much by one's social and cultural environment. No one ever tried to deny that Jesus worked miracles. What they did do was accuse him of using the power of Satan because he did miracles of healing on the Sabbath and thus, according to his opponents, broke the Law. Their argument was that no one could use the power of God to break the Law. Jesus, however, claimed that the Law must be understood anew and from the perspective of the advent of the kingdom of God.

The Gospel writers intended the miracles of Jesus to be understood theologically and spiritually, not historically and factually. In other words, the real meaning of Jesus's miracles can never be attained by merely substantiating their historicity. Their real meaning lies below the surface of the action and can only be explained theologically. Because of this, the Gospel writers never focus on the event itself. We get to see what leads up to the action and what follows from the action, but there is no dwelling on the action itself. The literary structure of miracle stories can be seen in miracles of healing. First, a sickness is described. Second, the sick person and Jesus encounter one another. Third, Jesus effects a healing. Fourth, the one healed demonstrates that he or she has been healed. Fifth, the people witnessing the healing are amazed. Note, too, that miracles are not something that Jesus does spontaneously or impulsively. As the Gospel of Mark makes clear, when Jesus is rejected by his own hometown, there is a need for a faith response on the part of the recipients before he will mediate the power of God and bring about a miracle. "And he could do no deed of power there.…And he was amazed at their unbelief" (Mark 6:5–6).

The context for understanding the miracles of Jesus is most often the Old Testament. Jesus's miracles are rooted in Old Testament imagery. This imagery helps connect the actions of Jesus with the primordial plan of God, showing how Jesus fulfils that plan. Jesus brings order out of chaos by healing the sick, expelling demons, and controlling the forces of nature. Jesus miraculously feeds the hungry not only with bread but with his very self. He rejects the social and religious taboos that marginalized women, ostracized the so-called unclean, and excluded people from God's salvation. Jesus proclaims the advent of the kingdom of God, which offers believers the hope of new life both in the present age and in the age to come.

The real value and richness of the Gospel miracle stories is to be found in their inner meaning. Those who choose to understand these stories from the question of what really happened will always remain on the outside. They will stress the external wonder, but always at the price of the internal meaning. It is precisely the internal meaning of these miracle stories that can and does relate to our own real-life experiences. We do not need more religious entertainment, strange wonder-causing events, or tales from the beyond. What most humans desire is to be made whole in all ways. Time and again we experience that, on our own resources, human wholeness is an impossibility. The miracles of Jesus are stories designed to inspire us with the hope and the good news that through faith and the power of God working through Jesus we can indeed be made whole.

NOTES

This chapter is reprinted with permission from *Review for Religious* 65 (2006): 202–5.

6

UP AGAINST CAESAR

JESUS AND PAUL VERSUS EMPIRE

John Dart

The "kingdom" of God and "gospel" are usually thought of as terms unique to Christianity. And who else but Jesus was called not only "the Son of God" but also "Lord" and "Savior"? In fact, say biblical experts, these terms and concepts were already familiar to residents of the Roman Empire who knew them as references to the authority and divinity of the emperors, beginning notably with Caesar Augustus before the dawn of the first century.

Julius Caesar was assassinated on the Ides of March in 44 BC. When a comet was later visible on July nights, Octavius, the adopted son and heir of Julius Caesar, promoted the idea that it was a sign that the divine Caesar was on his way to heaven. When Roman law in 42 BC deified Julius Caesar, the status of Octavius, who took the name Augustus, was strengthened by adding the phrase "son of God." Poets celebrated the divinity associated with Augustus, and across the empire coins, monuments, temples, and artwork promoted the cult of Augustus and other emperors who adopted Caesar as an honorific title.

To many in the empire, Roman civilization brought stability and wealth. And the people were urged to have "faith" in their "Lord," the emperor, who would preserve peace and increase wealth. "In the Roman imperial world, the 'gospel' was the good news of Caesar's having established peace and security for the world," wrote Richard A. Horsley in *Jesus and Empire*.[1] Christians gave secular words associated with the empire a new meaning. The Greek word *parousia* referred to the triumphant arrivals of emperors into cities. In churches, it meant the expected return, or second coming, of the heavenly exalted Christ. Churches, literally "assemblies," were the Christian counterparts to the Roman *ekklesiai* where Caesar was celebrated, according to Horsley, emeritus professor at the University of Massachusetts at Boston. "Caesar was the 'Savior' who had brought 'salvation' to the whole world."

In that context, the Christmas passage in the Gospel of Luke has a subversive tone, says Horsley. Angels bring "good news" of joy "to all the people," because of the birth of a "Savior, who is the Messiah, the Lord." A heavenly multitude joins the angels in proclaiming "on earth peace among those whom he favors." For the Romans, peace was the militarily imposed *Pax Romana*, and it was already guaranteed by Rome. Horsley has been a pioneer among biblical scholars who have emphasized the anti-imperial, political strategies of the Jesus movement. He has been joined in recent years by a growing number of colleagues, including prolific authors N. T. Wright and John Dominic Crossan. The latter's recent book, coauthored with Jonathan L. Reed, *In Search of Paul*, is subtitled: *How Jesus' Apostle Opposed Rome's Empire with God's Kingdom*.[2]

About fifteen years ago, Horsley edited an influential book, *Paul and Empire*,[3] and started a "Paul and Politics Group" that met at annual sessions of the Society of Biblical

Literature (SBL). "We launched a serious consideration of Paul as [being] opposed to the Roman empire," he said. "But I think it was 9/11 and the Bush administration's invasion of Iraq that really provoked interest." At the 2004 SBL annual meeting, a new program unit on Jesus and the Roman imperial world attracted ten speakers and required overflow rooms.

The escalating attention to the biblical era empire has been amplified by the open lament of some ethicists, church leaders, and politicians that the United States has assumed aspects of an empire—complete with religious imagery to assure skeptics of its benevolent motives. Despite the many differences between ancient Rome and present-day Washington, a growing number of critics are eager to draw comparisons and note the historical irony—whereas the early church reconceptualized the meaning of empire, current leaders have invoked Christian language to support the American empire.

In October 2004 about two hundred Christian ethicists issued a statement "about the erroneous use of Christian rhetoric to support the policies of empire," as it was put by one signer, Glen Stassen, who holds an endowed chair at Fuller Theological Seminary. The statement declared that "a time comes when silence is betrayal." The Christian call to peacemaking has been co-opted, the group said, when "a 'theology of war' is emanating from the highest circles of American government; the language of 'righteous empire' is employed...[and] the roles of God, church and nation are confused by talk of an American 'mission' and 'divine appointment' to 'rid the world of evil.'"

Also in October 2004, Brazos Press published a collection of essays, *Anxious about Empire*, edited by Wesley Avram of Yale Divinity School.[4] Interviewed by the school's *Reflections* magazine, Avram likened the Republican convention to a megachurch where President Bush spoke from a pulpit. "You realize that he is using a kind of language that's so infused with religious symbols that one wonders how the church can speak, when its language is so taken over by the culture."

Only days before the November 2004 elections, Union Theological Seminary in New York held a two-day conference on analogies between the Roman Empire and the American one. "This conference will explore how the imperial presumptions of American power today can find resonance with early Christian resistance to the Roman Empire," said organizer Brigitte Kahl, professor of New Testament. Fewer than one hundred attendees were expected; three hundred showed up.

In opening remarks, Hal Taussig, a visiting professor at Union and a pastor of a United Methodist congregation in Philadelphia, said he found it "stunning" to consider how early Christianity adopted Roman imperial terms as its own. "We were not quite listening in the 1990s" when scholars like Horsley and Crossan, two speakers at the Union conference, were proposing that Jesus was crucified primarily for his political opposition to Roman rule. "It has taken us too long to get here." Taussig credited another speaker, Elisabeth Schüssler Fiorenza, with breaking new ground in 1985 with her commentary on the Book of Revelation. "She made it clear that it was a message of oppressed people" against Rome, he said. Those Revelation themes were also treated in *Unveiling Empire*, a 1999 book by Wes Howard-Brook and Anthony Gwyther.[5] They suggested that the author of Revelation, John of Patmos, wrote his visionary text to shake the complacency of the churches in Asia about the cult of Caesar as well as about Rome's economic exploitation, violence, and arrogance. "For him, Rome was not an order with which one could cooperate," they wrote. "It was, instead, an incarnation of 'Satan.' It was both a ferocious Beast and a seductive Whore."

Biblical scholar Walter Brueggemann, in a blurb for *Unveiling Empire*, praised the writers for their critique of the "contemporary preoccupation with apocalyptic" themes. Howard-Brook and Gwyther understand that the Book of Revelation is an exercise in ecclesiology. That is, how to be the church in the face of a powerful and seductive empire.

Some years before Revelation was written, Paul was sending letters to churches in Asia Minor and Greece to build up the Christ-rooted societies with an egalitarian credo, recognizing believers whether they were Greek or Jew, male or female, slave or free. These assemblies stood "in contrast to the hierarchical social relations" in the empire, Horsley wrote in *Paul and Empire*, a book deemed significant by Wright, a New Testament scholar and the former Anglican bishop of Durham. "Tom Wright was one of the first to pick up on that theme, and he has run with it," Horsley said in an interview.

In a lecture at Princeton's Center of Theological Inquiry, Wright, like Horsley, tried to anticipate the objections of those who doubt there is political protest in Paul's message. "It is important to stress, as Paul would do himself were he not so muzzled by his interpreters, that when he referred to the 'gospel' he was not talking about a scheme of soteriology. Nor was he offering people a new way of being what we would call 'religious,'" said Wright. "For Paul 'the gospel' is the announcement that the crucified and risen Jesus of Nazareth is Israel's Messiah and the world's Lord. It is, in other words, the thoroughly Jewish...message which challenges the royal and imperial messages in Paul's world."

Rome regarded itself as the fount of justice that flowed to all its conquered nations. A temple to the Roman goddess Justice was established in Rome in 13 BC and "justice" had already been celebrated as one of the virtues of Caesar Augustus, Wright noted. To be successful, he said, the gospel of the Christians had to be positive, not merely subversive: "It claims to be the reality of which Caesar's empire is the parody; it claims to be modeling the genuine humanness, not least the justice and peace, and the unity across traditional racial and cultural barriers, of which Caesar's empire boasted."

In his Letter to the Romans (13:1–7), however, Paul counseled believers to be subject to and pay taxes to the governing authorities, which he said were instituted by God. Wright and Crossan both think that such passages reflect Paul's strategic decision not to invite punishment with open defiance of the empire. Pauline scholar Neil Elliott wrote in *Paul and Empire* that within the rhetorical structure of Romans "these remarks have an important function: to encourage submission, for now, to the authorities, rather than desperate resistance" that would endanger Christian Jews in Rome who were recovering from earlier imperial violence.

But didn't Jesus, himself, on the question of paying taxes, advise inquirers to give to Caesar what was Caesar's and to God what was God's? For some scholars, Jesus's answer indicates that the kingdom of God can coexist with the Roman power structure. But Horsley and some others view Jesus's response as a clever, indirect way to foil his foes' attempt to entrap him. In Israelite tradition, everything belongs to God and nothing to Caesar, said Horsley in *Hearing the Whole Story: The Politics of Plot in Mark's Gospel.*[6]

One evident slap at Roman rule in Mark is the story of Jesus healing the demoniac that no one had the strength to subdue. Jesus asks the man's unclean spirit for its name. "My name is Legion; for we are many," replies the man, using the Latin word for a large unit of Roman troops. The demons beg Jesus not to send them out of the country, but instead into a herd of swine; when he obliges, they promptly rush down a steep bank into the sea. Horsley believes the symbolism is unmistakable: Jesus takes control of the Roman forces that have brutalized people and foretells the army's demise.

The Gospel episodes of exorcisms depict a power struggle "at three levels—the individual possessed, the spirit world where God is battling Satan, and by implication the political level," said Horsley at Union Seminary. "If God/Jesus is winning the battle at the spirit level, as manifest in his exorcisms, then Roman rule is about to be terminated." Roman rulers are the doomed "rulers of this age" in 1 Corinthians 2:2–8, but Paul may also have alluded to malevolent cosmic powers, scholars say. Paul lauds God's power and secret wisdom "decreed before the ages for our glory" over against the "wisdom of this age or of the rulers of this age, who are doomed to perish….None of the rulers of this age understood this; for if they had, they would not have crucified the Lord of glory."

If more scholars come to accept the thesis that many of the New Testament writers were arguing with Roman rulers and their collaborators, it does not necessarily mean they will conclude that Jesus was primarily a political reformer or social revolutionary. Such theories, when broached in the past, have tended to be discounted for lack of evidence. However, Horsley and Crossan, as well as Wright, argue that the long-standing desire in western countries to separate politics from religion has inhibited the view that Middle Eastern and Mediterranean religion and politics were as tightly enmeshed 2,000 years ago as they are today.

"Depoliticized views of Jesus have trouble explaining why" Jesus was crucified by the Roman governor in Judea and why another attention-getting figure in the mid-first century named Jesus (ben Hananiah) got off easy, Horsley said. This other Jesus also predicted doom for Jerusalem but was deemed simply crazy and was beaten and then released. Horsley suggests that the accusation that Jesus of Nazareth pretended to be "king of the Jews" in Mark's passion story indicates that the Romans believed he deserved "the tortuous death reserved for provincial rebels as well as slaves." Though the Lord's Prayer seeks forgiveness of sins, the petition also asks for God's kingdom to come and "focuses on the people's economic needs, concretely sufficient food and mutual cancellation of debts," said Horsley, explaining how the sociopolitical side of Jesus's message is downplayed.

Crossan, an emeritus professor at DePaul University, published extensively on the "historical Jesus" from 1991 to 1994 and summarized his conclusions in *Who Killed Jesus?*[7] "The kingdom of God movement was Jesus' program of empowerment for a peasantry becoming more steadily hard-pressed...through insistent taxation, attendant indebtedness, and eventual land expropriation, all within increasing commercialization in the booming colonial economy of a Roman empire under Augustan peace," he wrote. Jesus lived an alternative life of shared meals, itinerancy, and human contact without discrimination. "That was how God's will was to be done on earth as in heaven," Crossan said.

Crossan and recent coauthor Reed, interviewed together at the University of La Verne in California, where Reed teaches, agreed that "kingdom of God" was a phrase chosen by Jesus to confront the divine Roman Empire. "Jesus could have talked about the community of God or the people of God," said Crossan. "Or the family of God, the synagogue of God," interjected Reed. "But as soon as you say the kingdom of God, you're taking over Roman terminology," added Crossan. "Jesus picked the one term that was really going to raise eyebrows."

Their book may in turn raise the eyebrows of some scholars. "I know we will get the accusation that it lacks spiritual content because it is too political," said Reed. "However, this is one of the few books on Paul that takes his ecstatic experiences seriously; there is a spiritual component to Paul." Crossan added, "People have no problem with the statement, 'Not Caesar, but Christ, is Lord.' That's fine. But then we say, 'Here's Caesar's program and here's Christ's program.' Now we are getting into politics." Asked what will happen if they relate their historical work to twenty-first-century politics, Crossan replied, "Then it will be called partisan politics."

Nonetheless, in both their book and the interview, the coauthors emphasized that they think neither the Roman Empire nor the U.S. empire can be called "evil." The early Christian conflict with Rome came because Rome "represented what we call 'the normalcy of civilization,'" said Crossan, noting that civilizations can be beneficial as well as unjust and oppressive. "So Paul's language about a 'new creation'—starting all over again—has to be taken seriously, because we're trying to get to a nonviolent civilization, and we don't have a clue what that looks like."

The Roman Empire, they wrote, was based on faith in achieving peace through military victory. Opposing the Roman philosophy, Paul the Jew followed in Jesus's footsteps by proclaiming a covenant of nonviolent justice and true peace. Crossan and Reed were asked to what extent America can embody those Christian ideals. They agreed that inasmuch as Rome was the greatest preindustrial empire and the United States is the greatest postindustrial one, "Paul's challenge is as forceful now as it was then."

NOTES

This chapter is reprinted with permission from *Christian Century* 122, no. 3 (2005): 20–24.

1. (Minneapolis: Fortress, 2003).

2. (San Francisco: HarperSanFrancisco, 2004).

3. (Harrisburg, PA: Trinity Press International, 1997).

4. (Grand Rapids: Brazos, 2004).

5. (Maryknoll, NY: Orbis, 1999).

6. (Louisville: Westminster John Knox, 2001).

7. (San Francisco: HarperCollins, 1995).

7

THE STUDY OF WOMEN IN THE EARLY CHURCH

Carolyn Osiek, RSCJ

In popular view, it is probably the success of the best-seller *The Da Vinci Code* that has raised new questions from millions of avid readers about women in the early church, especially Mary Magdalene. Its fast-moving sleuth tale continues to sell and, unfortunately, its wildly inaccurate historical interludes are included. But for historians, theologians, and biblical scholars, the real story is even more exciting and more complex. What follows is a brief recap of what is being discovered, and the questions and problems that remain, in the study of women in the early church.

MATERIAL EVIDENCE

Let's start with the things we can see and touch, what archaeologists and historians call "material culture." Though much visual art (such as paintings) has not survived, still some of it has. For example, in places like Pompeii and Herculaneum the catastrophic eruption of Mount Vesuvius on August 24 in the year 79 preserved many houses with furniture and artwork intact. Here we not only see women depicted in both mythological and everyday scenes, but also what women wanted painted on their walls and how they decorated their homes. Women's jewelry has been preserved, especially in burial contexts throughout the Mediterranean world. Both objects of adornment and of practical use were often buried with the deceased; for example, weapons with men, perfume bottles with women, dolls with children. As we gaze upon these items, we seem to have some kind of direct contact with their owners.

Sculpture gives us images of the people themselves, often idealized, but Roman art quite often renders realistic portraits, even down to skin blemishes and the effects of aging. There are also the so-called mummy portraits from Lower Egypt, paintings of real people that adorned their sarcophagi when they died. Here we see men, women, and children, Egyptian elites of mostly Greek descent, and we are then better able to visualize what other Eastern Mediterranean people, such as biblical characters, may have looked like.

The elements of material culture that reveal most, not only about people themselves but also about their relationships, are funerary inscriptions left on sarcophagi, marble tablets, and other forms of commemoration. Sometimes the language is conventional; for example, when a husband states that he lived so many years with his wife *sine ulla querella*, "without a quarrel," one suspects this is not literally true! But the depth of loving relationships is also felt in a husband's commemoration of a young mother who died in childbirth, or that of grieving parents of a deceased child.

SOCIAL HISTORY

It is often said that when men recount history, it is the story of wars. How many of us remember our history books of modern Europe or the United States as accounts of a series of wars with brief intervals of scientific and social progress? With few exceptions, in the past women have not waged war, but they have always been its victims, even as they still are today. One of the recent developments that has spread across the disciplines of history and archaeology is greater interest in what is called "social history," that is, not the story of politics and armed conflict, but of civic and family life. Those involved in social history are interested not so much in politics and wars as in social structures. How were families organized? How did they educate their children? How did they understand and celebrate birth, marriage, and death? What part did women play in public life and decision making?

In archaeology, too, it is no longer sufficient to excavate the large public buildings of an ancient city and ignore residential areas as of no interest. The excavation of housing is usually more difficult because building materials were not as sturdy as those used for public structures. Yet investigation of residential quarters has yielded enormous amounts of information about daily life, such as arrangement of rooms in a house and their distinctive uses, sources of water, cooking utensils, diet, and personal objects like combs, locks, and coins. Once gathered, this data must then be carefully interpreted.

During the past generation, there has been rapidly increasing interest in Roman social history, which forms the backdrop for the social history of New Testament people and those who immediately succeeded them. Thus, more information has been available, and more interest has been stimulated, to pursue study of the Jewish and early Christian family.

All of this new interest in social history has meant more evidence for the lives of women, and more interest in those lives. Inevitably, charting family life means charting women's lives and women's chief concerns. Because nearly all history and literature in the past, including the Bible, was written by men, men's perspectives and accounts of their experience prevails in the written record. Even stories told about women who are active in public life, such as Miriam's triumphant song (Exod 15:20–21) or the heroic actions of great women like Esther or Judith, have been filtered through the thoughts and expectations of male writers. In the New Testament, stories of faithful women disciples and those who encounter Jesus and go away cured hold our attention, but we realize again that these are not stories told by women, but by men about women.

GENDERED SPACE

In most cultures, including our own, there are definite differences in the subcultures of men and women. The things that men talk about and enjoy doing together are usually quite different from what women talk about and do together. If this is true today in our society, it was no less true two thousand years ago in the lands of the Mediterranean. What is preserved for us in the official record is public culture that is essentially male. The lives, joys, sorrows, and pastimes of women are largely inaccessible to us, except in furtive glances: personal objects and sometimes the details of stories. Comparison with present-day traditional societies, through the tools of cultural anthropology, often proves enlightening about what social structures and expectations were likely to have been current in similar societies thousands of years ago.

Social historians speak of "gendered space," delineating those areas of public space and private house that are predominantly occupied by either men or women. In the lands of the New Testament it was generally understood that the marketplace and law courts were men's space, while the house was the world of women. This does not mean that women were never in the marketplace or that men were never at home, but it does set certain areas apart conceptually as belonging to one gender or the other. One of the consequences of assigning the house to women is that they were expected to take complete control of its management. Thus people of both sexes arriving in a house that hosted the meeting of a house church, such as that of Prisca and Aquila (Rom 16:5), were setting foot in a space that was nominally controlled by the "master of the house," but was really the domain of his wife.

In the New Testament perhaps we catch a glimpse of the life of a group of widows living in their own space in the story of Tabitha/Dorcas (Acts 9:36–41), in which the deceased Tabitha is lamented by the whole group, who show Peter the garments she used to make for them. In this brief reference, we see the common plight of widows who band together for mutual support. Tabitha may well have been their patron, a wealthier woman, probably herself a widow, who provided what the others in their poverty could not afford.

In the story of the Syro-Phoenician or Canaanite woman narrated by Mark and Matthew (Mark 7:24–30; Matt 15:21–28), we see the characteristically fierce determination of a mother to do all that she can for her sick daughter, even to the point of putting up with the insults she receives from this foreigner Jesus, who nevertheless is able to help her. The accounts of the various women at the tomb of Jesus on Easter morning, always led by Mary Magdalene, may have developed from stories the women told to other women at home about their experience there. In narratives like these, even though they have come down to us through men's eyes and pens, still we can see something of the lives of women on their own terms.

FINDING THE VOICES OF WOMEN

Previously we have been talking about the use of the material and social sciences to "reconstruct" women's lives. Once that process has begun, it is open to interpretation from many angles. What we discover is only as good as the questions we ask. We need to ask new questions in order to find new answers. "Women should keep silent in the churches" (1 Cor 14:34) has become not only a prescription for church behavior but for all of life, as the voices of women are silenced in the telling of history.

If we begin from the assumption that the past story of women has been subject not only to neglect, but to deliberate suppression in favor of the socially stronger voices of men, we will know where to look to find women's voices. Thus, the task of reconstructing the history of women involves finding those lost voices that could have spoken to us of lives lived in heroic silence or in active participation in public life. We look between the cracks of history to find them, necessarily calling on our own experience to help guide the way. Thus, for example, the scholar who is also a wife and mother will more readily raise the questions surrounding the issues of birthing and raising children in the world of antiquity and in the first Christian house churches.

WOMEN IN PUBLIC LIFE

All this talk about the private and silent lives of women should not lead to a conclusion that ancient Mediterranean women never participated in public life. Careful study of letters of the elite of Rome has shown the active participation of upper class women in politics, even though they neither could vote nor be elected to office. Yet a careful reading of the public inscriptions of some of the cities of Asia Minor (today's west coast of Turkey) reveals that elite women held priestly and civic offices that in most places were held only by men. Wealthy women all over the Mediterranean world participated actively in the patronage system as well, providing public monuments, buildings, meals for the needy, and personal help to those who asked.

In the early church, women leaders like Mary mother of John Mark and Nympha hosted a house church (Acts 12:12; Col 4:15), while the traveling deacon Phoebe functioned as patron for many, including Paul (Rom 16:1–2). In later years, women deacons and even a few presbyters assisted at baptisms, gave pre- and post-baptismal instruction to women, went on pilgrimage, and represented the church in business transactions.

A BRAVE NEW WORLD

Research on women in Mediterranean antiquity and thus in the biblical world and the Bible itself is just beginning. We can look forward to many years of new discoveries to supplement the immense and growing pool of knowledge, most of which has been acquired in the past fifty years. It is in this context that the elusive figure of Mary Magdalene has emerged in recent years as disciple and apostle. While *The Da Vinci Code* may titillate with its story of secret loves, the love she demonstrated in the biblical texts about her and the role she played in the proclamation of the resurrection of Jesus are far more real. She speaks to us across the ages as what she was: a woman of courage and faith.

NOTES

This chapter is reprinted with permission from *The Bible Today* 43 (2005): 277–82.

8

MISUSING JESUS

HOW THE CHURCH DIVORCES JESUS FROM JUDAISM

Amy-Jill Levine

The fact that Jesus was a Jew has not gone unrecognized. Libraries and bookstores are replete with volumes bearing such titles as *Jesus the Jew, The Galilean Jewishness of Jesus, Jesus and the World of Judaism, The Religion of Jesus the Jew, Jesus in His Jewish Context, The Jewish Reclamation of Jesus*, and four volumes (and counting) of *A Marginal Jew*. The point is more than simply a historical observation. Numerous churches today acknowledge their intimate connection to Judaism: connections born from scripture, history, theology, and, as Paul puts it, Christ "according to the flesh" (Rom 9:5).

Nevertheless, when it comes to the pew, the pulpit, and often the classroom, even when Christian congregants, ministers, and professors do acknowledge that Jesus was Jewish, they often provide no content for the label. The claim that "Jesus was a Jew" may be historically true, but it is not central to the teaching of the church. The problem is more than one of silence. In the popular Christian imagination, Jesus still remains defined, incorrectly and unfortunately, as "against" the Law, or at least against how it was understood at the time; as "against" the Temple as an institution and not simply against its first-century leadership; as "against" the people Israel but in favor of the Gentiles. Jesus becomes the rebel who, unlike every other Jew, practices social justice. He is the only one to speak with women; he is the only one who teaches nonviolent responses to oppression; he is the only one who cares about the "poor and the marginalized" (that phrase has become a litany in some Christian circles). Judaism becomes in such discourse a negative foil: whatever Jesus stands for, Judaism isn't it; whatever Jesus is against, Judaism epitomizes the category.

This divorcing of Jesus from Judaism does a disservice to each textually, theologically, historically, and ethically. First, the separation severs the church's connections to the scriptures of Israel—what it calls the Old Testament. Because Jesus and his earliest followers were all Jews, they held the Torah and the prophets sacred, prayed the psalms, and celebrated the bravery of Esther and the fidelity of Ruth. To understand Jesus, one must have familiarity with the scriptures that shaped him (or, as a few of my students will insist, that he wrote).

Second, the insistence on Jesus's Jewish identity reinforces the belief that he was fully human, anchored in historical time and place. This connection is known as the "scandal of particularity": not only does the church proclaim that the divine took on human form, it also proclaims that it took on this form in a particular setting among a particular people. The church claims that divinity took on human flesh—was "incarnated"—in Jesus of Nazareth. Therefore the time and the place matter. Christianity follows Jesus of Nazareth, not Jesus of Cleveland or Jesus of Mexico City; the incarnation dates to the first century, not the twenty-first.

Further, the Jewish tradition into which Jesus was born and the Christian tradition that developed in his name were "historical religions," that is, their foundational events took place in history and on earth, rather than in some mythic time and mythic place; they have a starting point and a vision for the future. To disregard history, to disregard time and place, is to be unfaithful to both Judaism and Christianity.

Historically, Jesus should be seen as continuous with the line of Jewish teachers and prophets, for he shares with them a particular view of the world and a particular manner of expressing that view. Like Amos and Isaiah, Hosea and Jeremiah, he used arresting speech, risked political persecution, and turned traditional family values upside down in order to proclaim what he believed God wants, the Torah teaches, and Israel must do. This historical anchoring need not and should not, in Christian teaching, preclude or overshadow Jesus's role in the divine plan. He must, in the Christian tradition, be more than just a really fine Jewish teacher. But he must be that Jewish teacher as well.

Further, Jesus had to have made sense in his own context, and his context is that of Galilee and Judea. Jesus cannot be understood fully unless he is understood through first-century Jewish eyes and heard through first-century Jewish ears. The parables are products of first-century Jewish culture, not ours; the healings were assessed according to that worldview, not ours; the debates over how to follow Torah took place within that set of legal parameters and forms of discourse, not ours. To understand Jesus's impact in his own setting—why some chose to follow him, others to dismiss him, and still others to seek his death—requires an understanding of that setting. If we today have difficulty fathoming how our grandparents could function without the Internet and cell phones, let alone without television, how can we possibly presume to understand the worldview of Jesus and his contemporaries without asking a few historical questions?

When Jesus is located within the world of Judaism, the ethical implications of his teachings take on renewed and heightened meaning; their power is restored and their challenge sharpened. Jews as well as Christians should be able to agree on a number of these teachings today, just as in the first century, Jesus's followers and even those Jews who chose not to follow him would have agreed with such basic assertions as that God is our father, that God's name should be hallowed, and that the divine kingdom is something ardently to be desired. Jesus does not have to be unique in all cases in order to be profound.

Jesus's connection to Judaism can be seen not only in his general comments about Torah but also in his practice of its commandments. For example, Jesus dresses like a Jew. Specifically, he wears *tzitzit*, "fringes," which the Book of Numbers enjoins upon all Israelite men, which a number of Orthodox Jewish men still wear, and which can be seen today most readily in the *tallit*, or "prayer shawl," worn in the synagogue during worship. Numbers 15:37–40 reads, "The Lord said to Moses, 'Speak to the Israelites, and tell them to make fringes on the corners of their garments throughout their generations and to put a blue cord on the fringe at each corner. You have the fringe so that, when you see it, you will remember all the commandments of the Lord and do them, and not follow the lust of your own heart and your own eyes. So you shall remember and do all my commandments, and you shall be holy to your God.'"

These *tzitzit* may be compared to WWJD bracelets. Just as the bracelets remind their Christian wearers to ask, "What would Jesus do?," so the fringes remind Jewish wearers of all 613 commandments, or *mitzvot* (Hebrew; singular, *mitzvah*). The Gospels do not shy away from the fact that Jesus wore these fringes: it was these fringes that the woman with the twelve-year hemorrhage affliction touched in hopes of being healed, according to the account in Matthew 9:20–22.

Similarly, Mark 6:56 says, "And wherever he went, into villages or cities or farms, they laid the sick in the market-places, and begged him that they might touch even the fringe of his cloak, and all who touched it were healed." The fact that Jesus, according to Matthew 23:5, criticized the Pharisees and scribes because "they make their phylacteries broad and their fringes long" suggests that his phylacteries were narrow and his fringes shorter. Jesus does not dismiss Torah; to use modern idiom, he wears it on his sleeve.

The reminder of the fringes has a practical payoff for Christians. The Gospels' preservation of this detail indicates that the Old Testament must be acknowledged as more than just an anticipation of the coming of the messiah—as more than a book that can now be discarded or, more respectfully, put on the shelf next to the other antiques, to be admired but not used. By preserving the fact that Jesus wore fringes, the New Testament mandates that respect for Jewish custom be maintained and that Jesus's own Jewish practices be honored, even by the Gentile church, which does not follow those customs.

Not only did Jesus dress like a Jew; he ate like a Jew as well. He kept kosher; that is, he kept the dietary requirements established in Torah. Leviticus 11:3 is explicit about what animals are permitted for human consumption: "any animal that has divided hoofs and is cleft-footed and chews the cud"; thus the pig, the camel, the rock badger, and the hare are not kosher. Jesus would never have consumed a ham sandwich. Nor, by the way, would the occasion often have presented itself—archaeological investigation finds few pig bones in Galilee.

The only contact Jesus had with pigs is described in its most complete form in Mark 5:1–20. Following their expulsion from a severely possessed man, a group of demons so numerous that their former host identified himself as "Legion, for we are many," requested that Jesus send them into a herd of swine. Jesus agreed, "and the unclean spirits came out and entered the swine; and the herd, numbering about 2,000, rushed down the steep bank into the sea, and were drowned in the sea." Mark's narrative anticipates the mission to the Gentiles, for the city of Gerasa, where the story is set, was part of the Decapolis, a league of ten predominantly Gentile cities, and the presence of the pigs is a less than subtle clue to the non-Jewish composition of the population. The story also allows a political dig against Rome, given that the "unclean spirits" identify themselves as Legion, the Latin term for an army cohort. But as for Jesus's Jewish identity, neither he nor his Jewish associates would have mourned the loss of a herd of hogs—animals that are not kosher and that represent conspicuous consumption in that they cost more to raise than they produce in meat.

A critically aware, historically informed study of Jesus is also crucial to prevent the anti-Semitism that tends to arise when the history is not known. The concern to recover Jesus's Jewishness is particularly urgent these days. In churches and in the academy, in pronouncements made by Mexican Americans and Palestinians, women from Benin and men from Korea, the World Council of Churches and Catholic liberation theologians, Jesus's Jewishness is frequently erased. As Jesus continues to be the symbol for all that is socially good, many Christians depict his Jewish background as the epitome of all that is wrong with the world. If Jesus preaches good news to the poor, so the common impression goes, "the Jews" must be preaching good news to the rich. If Jesus welcomes sinners, "the Jews" must have pushed them away. If Jesus speaks to or heals women, "the Jews" must have set up a patriarchal society that makes the Taliban look progressive.

In the academy, certain schools of thought have managed to distinguish Jesus, whether implicitly or explicitly, from any sort of "Judaism." The popular push to depict Jesus as a Galilean and see Galilee as religiously and ethnically distinct from Judea winds up conveying the impression that "Judaism," with its Temple and its leadership, is quite distinct from the Galilean Jesus. The popular image of Jesus as a peasant often serves not to connect him to his fellow Jews but to distinguish him from them, since "the Jews" remain in the popular imagination not peasants but Pharisees and Sadducees or, in academic terms, members of the retainer and elite classes. Worse, the lingering view that Jesus dismissed basic Jewish practices, such as the laws concerning Sabbath observance and ritual purity, turns Jesus away from his Jewish identity and makes him into a liberal Protestant. My point is that any prejudicial commentary that divorces Jesus from Judaism and then uses the story of Jesus to condemn all Jews is not a Christian message.

NOTES

This chapter is reprinted with permission from *Christian Century* 123, no. 26 (2006): 20–25.

9

THE BIBLE, THE JEWS, AND THE PASSION

Eugene J. Fisher

Aweek or so before Ash Wednesday in 2004, the Committee for Ecumenical Affairs of the U.S. Conference of Catholic Bishops released a 150-page resource book for use by Catholic preachers, teachers, interested laity, and Catholic Jewish dialogue groups. Entitled *The Bible, the Jews and the Death of Jesus: A Collection of Catholic Documents*, the publication brings together excerpts and in some cases entire documents from various levels of Catholic teaching (the Second Vatican Council, Pope John Paul II, the Pontifical Biblical Commission, the Pontifical Commission for Religious Relations with the Jews, and the U.S.C.C.B. itself) pertinent to how the church reads its scriptures, understands its relationship with Jews and Judaism, and understands and presents its ever-deepening reflections on the saving mysteries of the passion and death of Christ, the one savior of humanity.

In his introduction to this collection, Bishop Stephen E. Blaire of Stockton, California, chairman of the committee, quotes from an address given by Pope John Paul II in 1997 to a group of Catholic, Protestant, and Orthodox Christian scholars assembled by the Holy See to study together "The Roots of Anti-Judaism in the Christian Milieu."

> Erroneous and unjust interpretations of the New Testament regarding the Jewish people and their alleged culpability have circulated [in the Christian world] for too long, engendering feelings of hostility toward this people. They contributed to the lulling of consciences, so that when the wave of persecutions swept across Europe…the spiritual resistance of many was not what humanity rightfully expected from the disciples of Christ. Your examination of the past, in view of a purification of memory, is particularly appropriate for clearly showing that anti-Semitism has no justification and is absolutely reprehensible.

Note the carefulness and clarity of the pope's words: "erroneous and unjust interpretations of the New Testament." These ancient errors in the interpretation of the passion narratives of the Gospels centered around the unjust and unjustifiable idea that "the Jews" (as opposed to some individual Jewish leaders) were and remained in subsequent generations collectively guilty for the death of Jesus. The Holy Father asserts that as embroidered over the centuries theological tomes, popular preaching, and passion plays contributed to the passive acquiescence and active participation of far too many Christians during the Holocaust. What, then, are some concerns raised by these documents that preachers, teachers, and those involved in creative presentations of the passion need to take into account?

1. *Theologically, responsibility for Jesus's death lies with the sins of all humanity, not just the particular Jews or Romans who were historically involved.*

The *Roman Catechism* (1566) of the Council of Trent is cited by the recent *Catechism of the Catholic Church* to underscore that "we cannot lay responsibility for the trial of Jesus on the Jews in Jerusalem as a whole...still less can we extend responsibility to other Jews of different times and places" (No. 597). The *Roman Catechism* stated, "Since our sins made the Lord Christ suffer the torment of the cross, those who plunge themselves into disorders and crimes crucify the Son of God anew in their hearts....Our crime in this case is greater in us than in the Jews. As for them, according to the witness of the Apostle, 'None of the rulers of this age understood this; for if they had, they would not have crucified the Lord of glory.' We, however, profess to know him. And when we deny him by our deed, we in some way seem to lay violent hands on him." Of all the historical actors, we are reminded, only Pilate is mentioned in the ancient creeds of the church.

2. *There must be an "overriding preoccupation to bring out explicitly the meaning of the Gospel text while taking scriptural studies into account."*

This means that it is not enough to say that a given passage is "in the Bible." Any single depiction will inevitably involve a selection from the four Gospels mixed with historical and artistic, creative elements. It is here that the old passion plays tended to create the illusion of collective guilt, for example, by depicting Jesus as opposed to Judaism, of which he was, rather, a devout adherent throughout his life. Indeed, Jesus submitted himself to the Law (Gal 4:4), extolled respect for it (Matt 5:17–20), and invited obedience to it (Matt 8:4).

3. *The presentation of Judaism must be nuanced.*

There were many different groups and movements in first-century Judaism, as there are today: Sadducees (supporters of the Temple priesthood), Zealots (revolutionaries against Rome), apocalypticists, Herodians, Hellenists, scribes, sages, miracle workers, and Pharisees of various schools of interpretation of the Law, ranging from the strict (for example, Shammai) to the more lenient (Hillel). Jesus is often depicted in the Bible in dialogue with the Pharisees, whose views on many things, such as a final divine judgment and the resurrection of the dead, Jesus shared. Many of his teachings on the Law were quite similar to those of Hillel, for example, whose followers would scorn the Shammaites as hypocrites and legalists, as did Jesus. In Luke, Pharisees try to warn Jesus against going to Jerusalem because of a plot against his life by the followers of Herod. It is likely that the sympathy for Jesus represented by Joseph and Nicodemus would have been shared by other Pharisees as well. The Synoptic Gospels (even Matthew, whose polemic against the Pharisees is the strongest) do not have them playing a role in Jesus' arrest or trial, only the chief priests and various "scribes and elders."

4. *Positive images of Jews and Judaism from scripture should be as or more plentiful than negative ones.*

Jews should not be portrayed as money greedy or bloodthirsty, for example, by changing the small "crowd" in Pilate's courtyard into a teeming mob. The Gospels clearly describe Jesus as being arrested at night because he was popular with the Jews, and in Luke, the women of Jerusalem weep as he is carrying his cross. Scenes of Jesus praying with his fellow Jews in synagogues, sharing the Passover Seder with them, and so on, will be helpful. Staging and costuming likewise need careful scrutiny: Are Jewish characters made to look dark and ominous over against Jesus and his followers?

5. *The role of Pilate needs to be approached with great care.*

Matthew and John, among the Gospels, seem to portray Pilate as a vacillating administrator who would have freed Jesus but for the manipulations of Caiaphas, the chief priest. While not exonerating Caiaphas (who is remembered in Jewish history negatively as a collaborator with Rome), other data from the Gospels and ancient secular sources such as Philo and Josephus portray Pilate as a ruthless tyrant. The Roman governor held absolute power over the chief priest, whom he appointed. When Pilate was called back to Rome, likely because his extreme cruelty (e.g., crucifying hundreds of Jews at a time without trial; see Luke 13:1–4) was stirring rebellion, Pilate's successor immediately deposed and replaced the chief priest. The Gospels agree that in Roman eyes Jesus's crime was that of political sedition against Rome, crucifixion being the Roman form of punishment for treason, a charge made explicit by the mocking sign "King of the Jews" nailed to the cross.

6. *There is, then, room for more than one dramatic style in depicting the role of Pilate and the chief priests while being faithful to the biblical and historical records.*

It needs to be made clear that Christ went freely to his death to save us all from the death of our sins, and that while some authorities of the Jews and those who followed their lead pressed for the death of Christ, what happened in his Passion cannot be blamed upon all the Jews then living, without distinction, nor upon the Jews of today. Although the church is the new people of God, the Jews should not be presented as rejected by God or cursed, as if such views follow from Sacred Scripture. All should take pains, then, lest in catechetical instruction and in the preaching of God's word they teach anything not in harmony with the truth of the Gospel and the spirit of Christ" (*Nostra Aetate*, No. 4).

It is impossible to overstate the importance of the church's call to Catholic preachers and teachers to exercise an "overriding preoccupation" with getting the Gospel accounts of Jesus's arrest, passion, and death just right. The condemnation of the charge of collective guilt against the

Jews was one of the most dramatic and theologically significant moments of the Second Vatican Council. Making it clear that it is our sins, not those of the individual actors in the events themselves, that bear the responsibility for Jesus's death, lies at the very heart of the Christian proclamation of the Gospel. Both Christians and Jews involved in the dialogue rightly understand that removing once and for all the ancient charge of "deicide" is the litmus test for the integrity of all our efforts, on both sides, since the council to bring about the reconciliation of the church with God's people, the Jews.

NOTES

This chapter is reprinted with permission from *America* 190, no. 5 (2004): 7–9.

10

TELLING THE TERROR OF THE CRUCIFIXION

Barbara E. Reid, OP

O f all the "texts of terror" in the Bible, the one that stands out most vividly is the crucifixion of Jesus. It is at the very center of the Christian story and is told over and over in our liturgies, our classrooms, and our faith sharing. The evangelists narrate Jesus's execution in the sparsest language. They provide very few details, stating simply, "and they crucified him" (Mark 15:24). We do not know whether the evangelists thought there was no need to give the details since everyone in those days knew what was involved in crucifixion or whether it was too terrible to describe, or too gruesome to be spoken of in polite assemblies. What we do know is that the Gospel writers are not so much interested in telling what happened as what it means. Each evangelist, along with Paul and the other New Testament writers, gives theological explanations to help faith communities understand what God was doing in the life, death, and resurrection of Jesus. These explanations are meant to instill hope, but under certain conditions some of them can turn the passion story into one that terrorizes. This chapter will explore briefly some of the theological explanations for the death of Jesus, examining their potential for terror or for hope.

A LIFE SACRIFICED FOR OTHERS

The most prevalent interpretation in the New Testament is that Jesus's death was a sacrifice for us. Paul speaks of Jesus's "sacrifice of atonement" (Rom 3:24), alluding to the ritual performed each year on Yom Kippur (Day of Atonement) in which the mercy seat, the top part of the ark of the covenant, was sprinkled with blood to atone for the sins of the people (Lev 16:14–16). Just as the blood of Temple sacrifices cleansed impurity from the Israelites, so Jesus's sacrifice freed human beings from sin and death. Paul also speaks of Jesus's death as "redemption" (*apolytrōsis*, Rom 3:24), a word that refers to the buying back of the freedom of a slave or captive. Jesus's death, then, purchases freedom from sin for humanity. Similarly, there is a saying in Mark 10:45 in which Jesus explains that he came "not to be served, but to serve, and to give his life as a ransom (*apolytrōsis*) for many."

In other texts (Gal 3:13; 2 Cor 5:21; John 11:50) Jesus is likened to the scapegoat onto which the sins of the people were symbolically transferred on Yom Kippur before it was driven out into the wilderness (Lev 16:10). Just as the guilt of the people is transferred to the innocent goat and the purity of the scapegoat is transmitted to the people, so Christ exchanges status with sinners. Also in this vein, Paul casts Jesus as a martyr or model of heroic death. He says, "Indeed, rarely will anyone die for a righteous person—though perhaps for a good person someone might actually dare to die. But God proves his love for us in that while we were still sinners Christ died for us" (Rom 5:7–8). Another related image is that of a silent lamb led to the slaughter. Mark particularly portrays Jesus as similar to the Servant in Isaiah 40—55 who endures beatings, buffets, spitting, and humiliation, on whom the guilt of the whole people was laid. Unjustly persecuted, he utters nary a word in protest, standing silent before his accusers.

TERRORIZING INTERPRETATIONS

Each of the above metaphors explains Jesus's death as a life sacrificed for others. While there is potential for this interpretation to be freeing, it can also be one that terrorizes when it functions to keep people who are servile in positions of subservience. Consider the story of a woman from rural Chiapas who tells how most of the women she knows have appropriated the Christian story:

> Jesus taught us how to sacrifice, how to give our lives for others, how to be humble and not self-centered. We sacrifice especially for our children, for our husbands, for our families. When there is not enough food, we give the best portions to our children and husbands. We sacrifice so our children can go to school, selling whatever we can in the market. We do not follow our own desires, but offer up our lives in service for theirs....I get up at four o'clock every morning to get water and gather wood and start the fire for breakfast. I do all the housework and I work in the fields alongside my husband as well, with my youngest baby strapped to my back. I get no pay for any of my work; we women are completely dependent on what our husbands give us. At the end of the day, I keep tending the children and fix dinner. Afterward there is more work to prepare for the next day. I don't ever rest or have a day off. Who would carry out my responsibilities? God has made it this way, we have to be humble

and sacrifice for others. All the suffering we endure we accept as our way of carrying the cross.

We do not have to travel to Chiapas to hear such a disturbing description; many women throughout the world understand their lives in this way. The notion of a life sacrificed for others can be a terrorizing interpretation of the cross for persons who are in oppressive situations. Rather than freeing persons who are weighed down, such a theology can enmesh people who are abused in even deeper cycles of violence and victimization. It can lull persons who are victimized into a passive acceptance of every kind of suffering rather than helping them take action to stop abuse where possible. An alternate image from the Gospel of John is of help. In the Gospel of John, rather than stand silently before his abusers, Jesus, when struck on the face by the Temple guard and rebuked for answering back to the high priest, confronts him: "If I have spoken wrongly, testify to the wrong. But if I have spoken rightly, why do you strike me?" (John 18:23). This image of a truth-teller confronting injustice could be a powerful antidote to the silent sufferer to aid persons in abusive situations to take action toward their well-being.

A SPECIFIC KIND OF SUFFERING

Another important aspect to consider is what kind of suffering Jesus was referring to when he gave the directive to his disciples, "Any who want to be my followers must take up their cross" (Mark 8:34). In the Gospel context "cross" has a very specific meaning: it refers to the suffering that comes as a consequence of proclaiming and living the gospel. Not every kind of suffering inflicted unjustly is the cross. As some of the women in Chiapas have recounted, this insight has brought about a dramatic shift in their understanding and praxis. Through reflection on the Bible in groups with other women, many have come to identify with Mary Magdalene and the other Galilean women disciples. They reasoned: if these women could find other ways to care for their traditional duties and leave their homes to preach the gospel, then why not us? The cross, as they understand it now, is not submitting to verbal and physical abuse, but it is the hardship of walking for hours through the jungle to reach the women's meetings, or enduring slander and suspicion when they exercise their newfound ecclesial ministries.

FREE CHOICE

Another element that is extremely important is that of free choice. When women and other abused persons have suffering imposed on them, this is not properly "the cross." Again, the Johannine Jesus offers a different image: a friend who freely lays down his life for his friends out of love (15:13). Jesus asserts that no one takes his life from him; he lays it down of his own accord (John 10:17–18). He symbolically acts out this freely offered self-gift by washing the feet of his disciples, and he instructs them to do the same for one another (13:1–20).

One example of how this played out in a village in Chiapas is told by a woman whose husband would frequently beat her after getting drunk. One morning when her friends saw her bruised face they decided to act. Some thirty women came together to the house to confront the husband. These women had moved away from emulating the silent, suffering Jesus of Mark, and had become a community of friends who were ready to lay down their lives for their friend. In this particular instance, the result was a happy one, as the husband stopped drinking and ceased beating his wife.

OBEDIENT SON

Another popular interpretation of Jesus's death is that "the Father sent him to die." While this particular formulation is not found in the New Testament, it has been extrapolated from texts such as the parable of the vineyard owner, who sends his own beloved son after all the other servants are killed (Mark 12:1–12), or from the scene in Gethsemane where Jesus prays to God to let the cup pass him by, "yet not what I want but what you want" (Mark 14:36). Such an image of obedience and submission easily translates into husbands demanding submission from wives, masters from slaves, etc. (Col 3:18—4:1; Eph 5:21—6:9). To break through the potential terror of this image it is important to keep in mind that God did not send the Son to die, nor did God will Jesus to die. God sent Jesus in human form to gain fullness of life for everyone for all eternity (John 3:16; 6:39–40; 10:10). Jesus, ever attuned to God's will, was obedient to this mission for life, which culminated in his death.

FORGIVING VICTIM

In the Gospel of Luke there is a particularly powerful image of Jesus as the forgiving victim, who even in the moment of excruciating pain prays "Father, forgive them" (Luke 23:34). There is a liberating dimension to this image. The willingness of a victim to forgive is a key part of any process of reconciliation. But a too-hasty or oft-repeated forgiveness can also perpetuate cycles of violence. For example, when a woman who is consistently beaten by her husband forgives him again and again, the forgiveness can feed a deadly cycle of abuse that never ends. When forgiveness is accompanied by repentance on the part of the perpetrator and the removal of the conditions for the violence, then true reconciliation is possible.

A STORY OF HOPE

Most important is that when Christians tell the terrible story of the death of Jesus we do so from a resurrection faith that takes us beyond the terror into new life, hope, and joy—which we taste even now! When our interpretations of the execution of Jesus function to take crucified peoples of today down from their crosses, rather than drive the nails in deeper, then we are living in resurrection faith. As the Nobel Prize-winning Guatemalan poet Julia Esquivel says, we live "threatened with resurrection!" She describes the paradoxes of our Christian life:

> To dream awake,
> to keep watch asleep,
> to live while dying
> and to already know oneself
> resurrected![1]

NOTES

This chapter is reprinted with permission from *The Bible Today* 44 (2006): 225–30.

1. Julia Esquivel, *Threatened with Resurrection: Prayers and Poems from an Exiled Guatemalan* (Elgin, IL: Brethren Press, 1982), 63.

11

THE EMPTY TOMB

Gerald O'Collins, SJ

As Easter comes round, many wonder how to understand the resurrection of Jesus Christ and its message for us. His empty tomb can make believers hesitant and even mildly embarrassed. Are they being innocently orthodox or even naively realistic in accepting that several women found the tomb of Jesus open and empty on the first Easter day? Is the sign of the empty tomb so crudely physical that it has no place in an adult faith content to talk in more general terms of Jesus's victory over death?

I wonder whether the real problem here is not with the historical case for the empty tomb but with its meaning. As such scholars as Raymond Brown, SS, and others have shown, a reasonable argument can be mounted for the basic reliability of the empty tomb story. But the difficulty for many people may be with "What does it mean?" rather than with "Did it happen?" Until we appreciate the meaning of the empty tomb, merely historical arguments may seem somewhat fruitless and beside the point. What might the empty tomb of Jesus reveal about God and the divine activity on our behalf? How could the empty tomb trigger and shape human faith? In proposing some answers to these large questions, let me limit myself to the oldest account of the empty tomb, Mark 16:1–8.

At first glance, the spare eight verses that conclude Mark's Gospel do not look promising for any reflections on the divine self-revelation and the response it evokes, human faith. But these laconic lines do in fact prove rich for those seeking to understand how God is made known in the whole story of the death and resurrection of Jesus. These verses report a pair of elements that persistently shape God's self-manifestation: events (in this case, the divine action that has transformed the situation before the arrival of the three women) and words (the angelic proclamation). As the Second Vatican Council taught, revelation occurs "sacramentally," through the interplay of words and deeds ("Constitution on Divine Revelation," Nos. 2, 4, 14, 17). Moreover, three contrasts are built into the story: darkness/light, absence/presence, and silence/speech. They enhance the telling of the story.

In the first place, Mark's text contrasts not only the nighttime darkness (between the Saturday and the Sunday of the resurrection) but also the darkness that enveloped the earth at the crucifixion (15:33) with the light of the sun, just risen when the women visit the tomb (16:2). The three women go to the tomb with light streaming into the sky and with something they never imagined about to be revealed: God has definitively overcome darkness and death.

A preliminary hint of what will be revealed comes when the women "raise their eyes and see" that the enormous stone, which blocked the entrance to the tomb and their access to the body of Jesus that they intend to anoint, "has been rolled away" (16:4). From the form of the verb, the so-called theological passive, the attentive reader knows that God, while not explicitly named, has brought about what is humanly impossible—opening the tomb and raising the dead to new life. The women see the first glimpse of what God has done in the unexpected reversal of the dark situation of death and the vindication of the dead Jesus. Without yet being aware of it, the women find themselves confronted with the first disclosure of God's action in the resurrection.

A second contrast emerges once the women enter the tomb itself. The absence of Jesus's body is set over against his personal presence, mediated through an interpreting angel in the form of a white-robed "young man."

A third contrast pits the confident words of the heavenly figure ("He has been raised. He is not here. See the place where they laid him") against the silence of the women as they flee from the tomb. Its tripartite shape adds force to the announcement. The angel proclaims, first, the great truth that concerns everyone and will change the universe forever: "He has been raised." Then he turns to the setting in which he is addressing the women: "He is not here." Finally, he points to the specific spot in the tomb where the body of Jesus had been buried: "See the place where they laid him." Both the words of the interpreting angel and the silent flight of the women highlight the dramatic and numinous moment of revelation.

Let us consider further some of the details. When the three women enter the tomb, they do not find the body of Jesus but a "young man, dressed in a white robe, and sitting on the right" (16:5). His shining apparel is the traditional dress of heavenly messengers. Like the Old Testament figures who remain seated to deliver a judgment, the angel does not rise to greet the women but speaks with authority to deliver an astonishing message. At the sight of the angel, the women respond by being "greatly amazed"—a reaction that matches the normal biblical response to a theophany. After countering their startled reaction with a word of comfort ("Do not be amazed") and revealing the resurrection, the angel commissions them: "Tell his disciples and Peter that he is going before you into Galilee. There you will see him." But the women "fled from the tomb. For trembling and astonishment had seized them, and they said nothing to anyone, for they were afraid." Some commentators explain the silent flight of the three women as a disobedient failure. First the male disciples of Jesus failed, and now also the women prove to be disobedient failures. They break down and disobey the commission they have received from the angel. So Mark's Gospel is alleged to close with total human collapse.

But is such an explanation rooted in Mark's narrative? Does it miss something very important about divine revelation? Does it gloss over the difference between the "track record" of the male disciples from chapters 6 to 15 and the women's "track record" in chapters 14, 15, and 16?

Beyond question, the conduct of male disciples of Jesus starts deteriorating from Mark 6:52, where the evangelist states that they do not understand the feeding of the 5,000 and that their hearts are "hardened." Their lack of faith leads Jesus himself to reproach them with their failure to understand and believe (8:14–21). A little later, he reproaches Peter sharply for perpetuating Satan's temptations by refusing to accept the destiny of suffering that awaits his master: "Get behind me, Satan" (8:31–33). James, John, and the other male disciples soon prove just as thickheaded (9:32; 10:35–40). Judas betrays Jesus into the hands of his enemies. When their master is arrested in the Garden of Gethsemane, all the male disciples desert him (14:50). Peter creeps back and goes into the courtyard of the high priest while Jesus is being interrogated. But under pressure he twice denies being a follower of Jesus and then swears that he does not even know Jesus (14:66–72). No male disciple shows up at the crucifixion, and it is left to a devout outsider, Joseph of Arimathea, to give Jesus a dignified burial (15:42–47). The progressive failure of Jesus's male disciples—and, in particular, of the core group of the Twelve—begins at Mark 6:52 and reaches its lowest point in the passion story.

Meanwhile women have entered Mark's narrative (14:3–9; 15:40–41, 47). They function faithfully, as the men should have done but failed to do. The women remain true to Jesus to the end, and are prepared to play their role in completing the burial rites. The women have "followed" Jesus and "ministered" to him in life and in death (15:41). Does then the frightened silence with which they react to the angel's message express a sudden, unexpected collapse on their part? Those who endorse such a dismal explanation might reread Mark's Gospel and notice how from the very start (1:22, 27) people over and over respond to what Jesus does and reveals with amazement, silence, fear, and even terror (e.g., 4:40–41; 6:50–51). His teaching and miracles manifest the awesome mystery of God come personally among us.

In a detailed study, *The Motif of Wonder in the Gospel of Mark*,[1] Timothy Dwyer shows how "wonder" is a characteristic motif in Mark's Gospel, occurring at least 32 times. Covering "elements which express astonishment, fear, terror, and amazement," it is the proper reaction of human beings to the awesome presence and power of God revealed in the teaching, miracles, death, and resurrection of Jesus. Apropos of the three key terms in Mark 16:8—flight, fear, and silence—Dwyer appeals to earlier passages in Mark and other relevant texts to conclude that the terms do not always bear negative connotations. Far from being always defective and the antithesis of faith, "flight is a common response to confrontation with the supernatural." The reactions of trembling, astonishment, and fear in Mark 16:8, as Dwyer shows, "are consistent with reactions to divine interventions early in the Gospel," reactions that "co-exist with faith." As for silence, he illustrates how in biblical stories temporary silence can result from a divine encounter. The silence of the three women is best understood as provisional; in due time they will speak to the disciples. The women remained silent with inappropriate persons, "until their message could be passed on to the appropriate audience, the disciples."

To sum up: It is with flight, trembling, astonishment, silence, and fear that the women initially receive the angel's message about God's action in raising Jesus from the dead (16:6) and about Jesus's appearance(s) to take place in Galilee (16:7). But these are proper reactions to the climax of divine revelation that has occurred in the resurrection. God's action has transformed the whole situation. The women have experienced the death of Jesus and his burial; they expect to find a crucified corpse when they visit the tomb. Their intense response to the angel's word matches the awesome power of God, now disclosed in the greatest divine act in the Gospel of Mark. God has triumphed over evil, the divine kingdom is breaking into the world, and the victimized Jesus is known to have been finally vindicated as the Son of God.

In Mark's Gospel, the crucifixion and resurrection stand over against each other. But they also interpret and "reveal" each other and may never be separated. Mark exemplifies this mutual "illumination" through two juxtaposed statements which the interpreting angel makes to the three women: "You are looking for Jesus of Nazareth who was crucified," and "He has been raised." To that message about the resurrection of the crucified one, the women react appropriately.

Read this way, Mark's concluding eight verses yield a rich commentary on the divine self-revelation conveyed by the numinous wonder of the resurrection. The later Gospels of Luke and John were to fill out the picture of the divine revelation at the open and empty tomb by highlighting the outpouring of the Holy Spirit. They will press beyond the Easter revelation of the Father and the Son (found in Mark 16) to acknowledge the full, "trinitarian" disclosure of Father, Son, and Holy Spirit.

But Mark's empty-tomb narrative has already done its work by presenting, or at least hinting at, some major aspects of God's revealing activity and the fitting human response. Yes, the discovery of the open and empty tomb did happen, and Mark takes us some distance in giving an account of "what that means." In dramatically reversing the situation of Jesus's death, God has transformed the human condition and led us into the light of a new day that will never end. It is only to be expected that the three women in Mark's story react with hushed astonishment. There is a time to fall silent, as those friends of Gandalf do in *The Lord of the Rings* when the old wizard quite unexpectedly returns: "Between wonder, joy and fear they stood and found no words to say." With the holy women, we also need to pay silent homage to the awesome wonder of Christ's resurrection from the dead: the beginning of God's new creation.

NOTES

This chapter is reprinted with permission from *America* 188, no. 14 (2003): 13–15.

1. (Sheffield, UK: Sheffield Academic Press, 1996).

12

APOCRYPHAL GOSPELS

EARLY CHRISTIAN PIETY AND THE LEGENDARY JESUS

Christopher R. Matthews

Where in the Gospels do we learn about the miraculous circumstances surrounding Mary's birth to Anna and Joachim, or that Joseph made the cross from trees he planted in his garden, or about the two men who come down from heaven to assist the risen Jesus from the tomb on the first Easter day?

Such information is clearly not included in the four canonical Gospels found in the New Testament. Rather, it comes from some of the ancient apocryphal Gospels that did not become part of the Bible. The Greek term *apokryphos* means "hidden" and is used with reference to early Christian writings to designate noncanonical literature. The stories alluded to above are found in documents known as the *Protevangelium of James*, the *Gospel of Philip*, and the *Gospel of Peter*, respectively. In the early centuries, these and other apocryphal writings were quite popular among Christian believers.

THE GOSPEL AND THE GOSPELS

In the first Christian decades the Greek word *euangelion*, which we translate as "gospel," was not used to designate a kind of writing but rather referred to the "message" or "good news" about Jesus. Paul makes frequent use of the term in this latter sense in his letters (e.g., 1 Thess 1:5; 2:4; Gal 1:11; 1 Cor 15:1; 2 Cor 2:12; Rom 1:9; 15:19), which predate the appearance of the first Gospel book. An innovative development from the term "gospel" = "message of salvation" to "Gospel" = "book" may be traced to the opening verse of Mark's Gospel: "The beginning of the good news [*euangelion*] of Jesus Christ, the Son of God" (Mark 1:1). Other books included in the New Testament that tell the story of Jesus's life and teaching also came to be designated as Gospels (according to Matthew, Luke, and John), even though they do not name themselves as such. That this practice continued among numerous other writings composed in the second, third, and following centuries is clear from the references to them in various early Christian writings. Thus many early Christians had access to a wide array of Gospel-type writings beyond those that were eventually recognized as canonical.

THE PERSISTENCE OF APOCRYPHAL GOSPELS

Once a general consensus was reached in the fourth century that the twenty-seven books included in the New Testament alone were authoritative, those writings found on the other side of this canonical boundary were not preserved with the same degree of care as the documents recognized as scripture. Indeed, in many cases formerly popular but now suspect writings were suppressed as the term "apocryphal" took on the meaning "heretical" or "rejected" writings. Thus, although we know scores of titles of such ancient works because they are mentioned and/or quoted by various patristic authors or included in ancient lists of disputed writings, many of them did not survive. Even so, many noncanonical writings did endure, even in the face of official sanctions. Copyists considered them to be valuable and continued to include them in new manuscripts. Later ecclesiastical writers drew on them to produce new composite works preserving the legacy of an earlier time. Moreover, numerous scenes in the repertoire of Christian art down through the centuries drew their inspiration from narratives found only in apocryphal texts. Pictorial representations on church walls, windows, and other religious objects (e.g., sarcophagi) were a key way in which such traditions about Jesus, Mary, the apostles, and other saints was passed along.

THEOLOGICAL IMAGINATIONS: THEN AND NOW

One fundamental motivation for the composition of apocryphal Gospels was the desire of their audiences to know more about Jesus than the canonical Gospels tell us. This is not to rule out that in some cases an apocryphal Gospel may in fact preserve material independent from or older than that found in the canonical Gospels. Many scholars suspect that this may be the case with parts of the *Gospel of Thomas*, or with some of the apocryphal Gospels known only in fragmentary form. In other cases it is clear that the apocryphal texts are aware of the canonical materials and consciously seek to supplement them in an endeavor to fill in the "gaps" left by the earlier writings.

Just as early Christians were eager consumers of ever-expanding stories about Jesus and those closest to him, so modern people are fascinated by any ancient materials that purport to shed light on Jesus's "real story." Inquiring minds want to know! This sometimes leads to an unfortunate situation in which ancient documents, which are already truly fascinating in their own right, are sensationalized more in the pursuit of marketing coups than in the growth of understanding. This recurring circumstance has recently been illustrated in the case of the *Gospel of Judas*, which tells us nothing about the historical Judas or Jesus, but does illuminate the theological ruminations of certain second-century Gnostic Christians. Dan Brown's novel *The Da Vinci Code* exploits pieces of apocryphal lore taken willy-nilly from a diverse group of ancient gospels and other sources to construct a hypothetical counter-history to the "official" story of Jesus and the early church. While such liberties may be permissible in a novelistic endeavor, greater attention to the true nature of these ancient writings would have made it possible to present a compelling fiction without so many glaring historical absurdities.

THE TERRAIN OF THE APOCRYPHAL GOSPELS

Space allows no more than a selective overview of some of the chief categories of the various apocryphal Gospels, along with a brief account of one of the more intriguing texts.

JEWISH-CHRISTIAN GOSPELS

It is significant that "Jewish Christians," believers in Christ who continued to observe Jewish customs and practices, existed for centuries after the time of Jesus. Various references to and quotations from "Jewish-Christian Gospels" are found in the writings of such early church figures as

Clement of Alexandria, Origen, Eusebius, Epiphanius, and Jerome. In this case we are dealing with "lost Gospels," insofar as all that has come down to us are fragments, and uncertainty remains about the precise contours of such documents.

The *Gospel of the Nazareans*, which seems to date from the first half of the second century, was apparently similar to the canonical Synoptic Gospels. Some scholars suggest that it represents a paraphrastic rendering of the original Greek version of Matthew's Gospel into Aramaic. The material that survives includes interesting additions to and variations on the canonical accounts. According to Jerome, in this Gospel the death of Jesus is marked not by the rending of the temple veil (Matt 27:51) but by the collapse of its large lintel.

The *Gospel of the Ebionites* is also especially reminiscent of Matthew. It seems to have been known by Origen, Ambrose, and Jerome as the *Gospel of the Twelve* or the *Gospel according to the Apostles*. It too may date to the first half of the second century, was composed in Greek, and appears to know the canonical Gospels. According to Epiphanius, it begins with the baptism of John, perhaps indicating that it skipped over the birth of Jesus in correspondence with the Ebionite Jewish-Christian sect's denial of the virgin birth.

The *Gospel of the Hebrews* differs quite noticeably from the previous two items as well as from the canonical Gospels. Although it is written in Greek, perhaps early in the second century, it bears no relation to Matthew. It seems to have been an authoritative text for Jewish Christians in Egypt and reflects a theological understanding based on Jewish wisdom literature. Particularly noticeable is the prominent place given to James, the brother of Jesus, who is not only present at the Last Supper but is also the recipient of an appearance of the risen Jesus.

GNOSTIC GOSPELS

Among the ancient library of predominately Gnostic works discovered in Egypt at Nag Hammadi in 1945 are a number of texts called Gospels, including the *Gospel of Truth*, the *Gospel of Thomas*, the *Gospel of Philip*, and the *Gospel of Mary*—that is, Mary Magdalene. The Gnostics (the term derives from the Greek word *gnōsis*, "knowledge") made much of a secret or esoteric message of salvation that lay below the surface meaning of the ordinary Christian message. The Gnostic Gospels seem more focused on delivering this message (gospel in the original sense) rather than conforming to a literary genre. The *Gospel of Truth* in particular is probably better classified as a meditation than a Gospel. The *Gospel of Philip* presents an anthology of sayings and statements, with few contacts to the canonical tradition, that is primarily concerned with Gnostic sacramental teachings.

INFANCY AND PASSION GOSPELS

Early Christians wanted to know a great deal more about the circumstances of the Savior's birth and early life than could be learned from the infancy accounts in Matthew's and Luke's Gospels. Legendary stories developed to fill in the gaps in the canonical accounts with anecdotes about the holy child and his parents. Early examples are the *Protevangelium of James* and the *Infancy Gospel of Thomas*, while later examples include the *Arabic Infancy Gospel* and the *Gospel of Pseudo-Matthew*.

Corresponding to interest in the beginning of the life of Jesus are various later texts concerned with the events surrounding the passion, including the creedal assertion that Christ "descended into hell." The *Gospel of Bartholomew* understands the latter event to take place during the middle of the crucifixion, when Christ descends into hell to bring out

Adam and the patriarchs Abraham, Isaac, and Jacob. The *Gospel of Nicodemus*, also known as the *Acts of Pilate*, represents itself as Nicodemus's account of the events surrounding the passion of Jesus. It also includes a lengthy account of the descent of Christ into the underworld. Yet another version of the passion events as well as various consequences of the resurrection are found in the *Gospel of Gamaliel*.

GOSPEL OF PETER

The surviving narrative of the *Gospel of Peter*, which opens and closes in mid-sentence, purports to be Peter's firsthand report of the events surrounding Jesus's passion; it breaks off just as the account appears to be introducing a post-resurrection appearance of Jesus. According to Eusebius (*Hist. eccl.* 6.12.2–6), Serapion, bishop of Antioch from 199 to 211, knew of its use in the church of Rhossus and at first allowed it to be read. Subsequently he was informed of its heretical associations and wrote a treatise refuting false statements in it. In addition to evidence indicating that the *Gospel of Peter* was known in both Egypt and Syria before 200, parallels with passion traditions in the *Epistle of Barnabas*, Justin Martyr, and *Ascension of Isaiah* push its likely date of composition back into the period before 150.

Those who would place the *Gospel of Peter* in the second century point to its fantastic depiction of the resurrection of Jesus in 9:35—10:42 as a clear example of a popular sort of imaginative Christian literature that seeks to fill out the story of Jesus known from other sources. In the passage just mentioned, Jesus's tomb is under guard when the soldiers see two angelic figures descend from heaven. The stone blocking the entrance to the tomb rolls away of its own accord and the two enter the tomb. Subsequently they emerge, supporting a third figure whose head reaches beyond the heavens. These three are followed by the cross. When a voice from heaven inquires whether proclamation has been made to the dead, the cross answers, "Yes!" Analogous popular material is not entirely absent from the canonical passion narrative (see, e.g., Matt. 27:51b–53).

Those who would place the *Gospel of Peter* in the first century emphasize that, once stripped of novelistic features that have been added secondarily, it is possible to recognize in the scene just summarized the formal characteristics of an epiphany story, fragments of which may appear in Matthew's (28:1–4) and Mark's (16:1–8) narratives of the empty tomb as well as in the Synoptic accounts of the transfiguration of Jesus (Mark 9:2–8 parr.). No matter when it is dated, the *Gospel of Peter* exemplifies a wider phenomenon in early Christianity of apocryphal writings that invoked the name of Peter to authorize the transmission of their content.

CONCLUSION

The apocryphal Gospels preserve a valuable heritage that enables scholars to understand the social and theological history of early Christianity, and especially its popular piety, to a degree not possible without these documentary resources. While the apocryphal Gospels may not shed much light on the life, teachings, and significance of the Jesus of history, they do tell us something about those who seek to know more about such things, both then and now.

BIBLIOGRAPHY

Modern collections of Christian apocryphal writings in English translation with introductory material are available in the following standard reference works:

Elliott, J. Keith. *The Apocryphal New Testament: A Collection of Apocryphal Christian Literature in an English Translation.* Oxford: Clarendon Press, 1993.

Schneemelcher, Wilhelm, ed. *New Testament Apocrypha.* Rev. ed. Vol. 1, *Gospels and Related Writings.* Louisville: Westminster/John Knox, 1991.

A more popular summation of such materials as they relate particularly to Jesus and his closest associates may be found in:

Elliott, J. Keith, ed. *The Apocryphal Jesus: Legends of the Early Church.* New York: Oxford University Press, 1996.

For the influence of Christian Apocrypha on Christian art, see:

Cartlidge, David R., and J. Keith Elliott. *Art and the Christian Apocrypha.* New York: Routledge, 2001.

Gnostic Gospels may be found in:

Meyer, Marvin, ed. *The Nag Hammadi Scriptures: The International Edition.* New York: HarperOne, 2008.

NOTES

This chapter is reprinted with permission from *The Bible Today* 47 (2009): 153–59.

13

LECTIO DIVINA

BRIDGING THE GAP BETWEEN GOD'S HEART AND OURS

John Belmonte, SJ

Talk show host Jay Leno has a very funny segment on his *Tonight Show* where he interviews the "man on the street," testing people's knowledge in a given subject matter. Rare is the person who does well. On one occasion he asked questions about a topic that keenly interests me: the Bible. While the survey was hardly scientific, the questions were very basic. No historical-critical method here. "Name one of the ten commandments," Jay asked. "Freedom of speech," the man unhesitatingly responded. "Name the four Gospels," Jay asked. With a befuddled look the woman was unable to answer. "Name the four Beatles," Jay asked. Without any hesitation and a relieved smile, the woman responded, "John, Paul, George, and Ringo." My personal favorite was the man whom he asked, "In the Old Testament, who was swallowed by the whale?" He looked directly into the camera and, as serious as death, said, "Pinocchio."

As someone who has taught scripture to high school students, these answers did not surprise me. Religious educators and biblical scholars regularly decry a growing lack of familiarity with scripture. Catholic ignorance of the Bible is proverbial. A study of 508 teenagers by the Princeton Religion Research Center confirmed that Catholic young people are much less familiar with scripture than their Protestant counterparts. Even more distressing is the finding that thirty percent said that they never even opened the Bible. If Saint Jerome's axiom, "Ignorance of the Scriptures is ignorance of Christ," is true, then those of us who are full members of the Catholic Christian community have a serious situation on our hands. Isn't it incumbent upon us to pass on the tradition, to introduce others to the living God, to dispel ignorance of the Word of God? If not us, then who?

Even amid the decline in elementary biblical knowledge, help is on the way. Vatican II did much to help revive interest in scripture and one method that may help bridge the gap Mr. Leno so cleverly pointed out is the ancient monastic method of reading the Bible called *lectio divina*. The Latin expression *lectio divina* does not translate into English with great accuracy. Literally, it means "holy reading." Within the monastic tradition, and in Saint Benedict's Rule in particular, its meaning is obvious. *Lectio divina* is an attentive and in-depth reading of the sacred scriptures intended not simply to satisfy one's curiosity but to nourish one's faith. Benedict's monks were to nourish themselves with the divine food of scripture in order to have sufficient resources for the journey of faith. In the Rule of Saint Benedict, the monk is exhorted to listen carefully and willingly to holy readings, the *lectiones sanctas*. The reading is holy because its object is the word of God. Scripture is approached not for scientific or technical reasons but in order to deepen one's personal commitment to God and God's Son.

LECTIO DIVINA FROM THE MONASTERY TO THE MARKETPLACE

All quarters of the church, from official pronouncements to informal movements, have in recent times repeatedly affirmed the need for and effectiveness of *lectio divina*. There are many ways in which one can encounter God through the biblical word. Yet, the rich history, significant connection to tradition, genuine spirituality, and pastoral applicability of *lectio divina* make it a particularly attractive method.

Lectio divina is one instrument of grace by which we encounter Christ in the scriptures. When practiced every day, *lectio divina* fosters the kind of contact with God's word that, over the course of a lifetime, promises a life of prayer lived out in faithful love. To suggest that a specific method for *lectio divina* might be necessary carries with it a risk. In our practice of this method we might be tempted to follow rigidly the proposals offered as rules and not as suggestions. To do so would be a mistake. What *lectio divina* demands in the first place is an openness to the Spirit, which any master of the spiritual life would see as a prerequisite to prayer. Ignatius of Loyola's instruction in his Spiritual Exercises to those who intend to pray is a good example. He suggests that believers must always pray "with great spirit and generosity toward their Creator and Lord."[1] Balance and flexibility are very important as one begins to practice *lectio divina*. We should always avoid rigidity, excessive formalism, or forcing things. My intention is not that the suggested schema that follows be realized as a fixed program; *lectio divina* is a way to encounter God, and we should always feel free to utilize it according to our own rhythms, gifts, and desires.

Having pointed out the importance of some prerequisites to *lectio divina*, such as balance, openness, and flexibility, a word is in order about the structure or steps that this ancient practice usually takes. Much has been written about these steps, but the most exhaustive and perhaps best-known example comes from Guigo II (1115–1198), the Cistercian prior at Chartres from 1173 to 1180. In his "Letter on the Contemplative Life," also known as *Scala Claustralium*, Guigo gives the classic four-part expression to the *lectio divina*: *lectio, meditatio, oratio,* and *contemplatio*. Since Guigo's text has become a nearly obligatory point of reference for someone considering *lectio divina*, it seems appropriate to reproduce here a brief summary citation from the letter:

> One day during manual labor, as I was beginning to reflect on the spiritual exercise of man, suddenly four spiritual steps appeared to my mind: reading, meditation, prayer, and contemplation. This is the ladder of the monks by which they are elevated from the earth to heaven and even though it may be formed by only a few steps, nevertheless it appears in immense and incredible greatness. The lower part rests on the earth; however, the higher part penetrates the clouds and scrutinizes the secrets of the heavens.
>
> Now the reading consists in the attentive observation of the Scriptures with one's spirit applied. The meditation is the studious action of the mind, which seeks the discovery of hidden truth by means of one's own intelligence. The prayer consists in a religious application of the heart of God in order to dispel evil and obtain favors. The contemplation is an elevation into God, from the mind attracted beyond itself, savoring the joys of eternal sweetness....
>
> Reading seeks the sweetness of the blessed life, while meditation finds it. Prayer asks for it and contemplation tastes it. Reading, in a certain way, brings solid food to the mouth, meditation chews and breaks it up, prayer obtains its seasoning, contemplation is the same sweetness which refreshes and brings joy.[2]

Guigo sets down a four-part method, but for our purposes we will reduce that structure to three: *lectio*, *meditatio*, and *oratio*. The reason for collapsing the final two steps into one is simple. Prayer is at the core of the way the two final steps are conceived. By collapsing them into a third phase, we respect the progression that naturally develops from the first two steps. However, we leave open the possibility of expanding on the process of prayer by adding three more steps: *discretio*, *deliberatio*, and *actio*. Some critics object to any tinkering with the traditional structure of *lectio divina*. Even so, a brief look at the historical development of the method over the centuries shows that one can understand Guigo's four steps as an expression of the monastic world of his time. Our minor change should be viewed in the same light.

THE PRACTICE OF *LECTIO DIVINA*

The first thing necessary to practice *lectio divina* should be obvious: time. As with anything worth doing or any relationship worth maintaining, the practice of *lectio divina* must be worth spending time doing. While we should avoid the kind of rigidity described above, the spiritual life does demand a certain amount of healthy discipline. Whether we want to fix a regular time, a certain period, or the most effective time, regularity is important. Our time is a precious thing, and offering it to God is a very simple and concrete first step toward our meeting God in prayer.

Equally obvious but also quite necessary to consider is which text to use for *lectio divina*. Our emphasis in *lectio divina* remains squarely with the biblical text. It is possible to substitute other texts for biblical texts; however, we should not lightly forfeit the surpassing value of reading, meditating, and praying with what the Fathers called the *sacra pagina*. Jerome himself reminds us that "the text presents itself simply and easily in words, but in the greatness of its meaning, its depth is unfathomable."[3]

Related to our emphasis on the biblical text itself is the presupposition that *lectio divina* is a continuous reading of the whole Bible. In our practice of *lectio divina* we should avoid the temptation to select texts well suited to topics chosen in advance. By attending to the whole of scripture, as the liturgy does in the lectionary, we preserve the context of biblical revelation, both the Old and New Testament. We must avoid the risk of allowing the *lectio* to "overflow the riverbanks of the tradition and the church," as Cardinal Martini has written.[4] Practicing *lectio divina* within the context of the whole of biblical revelation emphasizes the unity of scripture and our belief in the Bible's inspiration by God. Moreover, emphasis on the unity of scripture allows us to avoid the temptation of placing scripture at the service of ideology or subjectivism.

Time set aside for God should take on a dimension different from the rest of one's day. To help mark that moment, most spiritual masters suggest that the person who sets out to pray begin by making some kind of *epiclesis*, which is an invocation or "calling down" of the Holy Spirit to consecrate. In the Eucharist, we call down the Spirit upon the bread and wine to transform them into the body and blood of Christ. As we begin *lectio divina* we should remind ourselves that it is through the work of God in the Spirit that the written word is transformed in our lives into the living word.

THE FOUR STEPS OF *LECTIO DIVINA*: *LECTIO, MEDITATIO, ORATIO, ACTIO*

Having set aside the time, "selected" the text, and invoked the Spirit, we are ready to begin the first formal step of *lectio divina*, called the *lectio*. This is the moment in which we read and reread a passage from the Old or New Testament, alert to its most important elements. The operative question is, What does the text say? Patient attentiveness to what the text has to say characterizes our stance before it. We should read the text for itself, not to get something out of it, like a homily, a conference, or a catechism lesson. The word of God should be allowed to emerge from the written word.

In *lectio,* each person's experiences and talents before the text come into play. The more experience or education one has, the more one will potentially bring to the text. Knowledge of biblical languages or an understanding of theology can also enrich one's reading. Consultation of available biblical commentaries or dictionaries can be especially helpful as we attempt to expand our understanding about what the text is saying. Paying attention to grammar, the usage of words and the relationships of verbs to nouns or of subjects to objects can make the text begin to take on new and unexpected significance.

The second step, called the *meditatio,* is equally important. We leave behind the specifics of the text and focus instead on what is behind it, on the "interior intelligence" of the text, as Guigo puts it.[5] The *meditatio* is a reflection on the values that one finds behind the text. Here one must consider the values behind the actions, the words, the things, and the feelings that one finds in a particular scriptural passage. Anyone who honestly seeks God and one's authentic self in prayer will hear the echoes of joy, fear, hope, and desire coming from the sacred page. The operant question for this stage doesn't stop at what the text says, but asks, What does the text say to me? We seek to make emerge from history and context the specific message of the text. The shift from external forms to internal content makes this stage an important one.

The *meditatio* is an activity that engages our intellect. As we pass from the second to the third stage of *lectio divina*, we move more into the realm of religious emotions. Remaining on an intellectual level can be safe and comfortable, but the goal of prayer is not knowledge about God, but God himself. In the *oratio* our imagination, will, and desires are engaged as we seek union with God. *Oratio* in its most fundamental sense is dialogue with God. Gregory the Great called it "the spontaneous meeting of the heart of God with the heart of God's beloved creature through the word of God."[6]

When we progress from *meditatio* to *oratio* an immediate experience of infused mysticism is hardly to be expected. Mystical union with God is not necessarily an ordinary part of Christian life. Nevertheless, the passage from *meditatio* to *oratio* is the vital and decisive moment of Christian experience. The more deeply we enter the *oratio*, the more we move beyond the text, beyond words and thoughts. The *lectio* is useful and the *meditatio* is important since they lead us to the *oratio*, which is life in its fullest sense, the life of Christ that he lives in the one who contemplates him. *Oratio* is the passage from the values behind the text to adoration of the person of Jesus Christ, the one who brings together and reveals every value. Unlike the *lectio* and *meditatio*, there is no operant question in the *oratio*. At its core, *oratio* is the silent adoration of the creature before the Creator, a rare and miraculous gift.

When the person who practices *lectio divina* reaches the level of *oratio*, it would seem that that moment would be conclusive. However, the dynamism of prayer that began during the *epiclesis* before the *lectio* is not interrupted here. To the contrary, it naturally continues and the *oratio*, as we are proposing it here following Cardinal Martini's insight, possesses its own steps, called *discretio, deliberatio,* and *actio*.[7] These three steps represent the way *lectio divina* is lived out in daily life. Given the growing dissociation of the faith from daily life, these three successive moments take on great significance.

Since the *meditatio* intends to put one in contact with the values of Christ, to encourage our identification with those things that are important to Christ, we naturally come to moments of decision. The *discretio* is the capacity that the Christian acquires through grace to make the same choices as Christ. Cardinal Martini describes *discretio* like this: "It is the discernment of that which, in a determined historical moment, is best for oneself, for others and for the Church."[8]

The second moment of the *oratio* is called the *deliberatio*. It is an interior act by which one decides in favor of the values of the gospel. One chooses to associate oneself with Christ and everything that association represents—in a word, discipleship. If the *discretio* is described as the capacity of a person to choose, then the *deliberatio* is the choice itself.

The final moment is called *actio*. In this final step, the choice we make in the *deliberatio* is given form and substance. Prayer becomes something more than simply setting aside time for God or an attempt to better ourselves. Our lives begin to take shape from the choices we have made as a result of prayer. The *actio* is the integration of a kind of apostolic consciousness that informs our choices so that we have made and lived our choices from our encounter with the living God.

Some critics would leave these last steps, particularly the *actio*, out of any proposed *lectio divina*. The addition of an extra step suggests perhaps overzealousness or even the influence of an "ideology of efficacy" regarding one's prayer. Too often, we feel we need to make prayer into something. However, in the face of a modern world in which the outward signs of the mystery of God are ever more difficult to recognize, where a daily experience of gospel or even transcendent values becomes harder to find, and where choices besiege one's conscience and stifle rather than uplift the Spirit, this criticism is unconvincing. If anything, the connection between prayer and our life choices should become more explicit, not less. The faith, hope, and love made manifest in the choices our lives become must be nourished by contact with the word of God.

CONCLUSION

Lectio divina is one graced instrument to bridge the gap that exists between our hearts and God's. As the faith risks being further dissociated from daily life, the simplicity and potential of a method like *lectio divina* take on greater significance. Firmly rooted in the church's tradition, it presumes careful attention to what biblical specialists are thinking and teaching. Rigorous study is complemented by disciplined meditation and prayerful contemplation of the word of God. Far from being an objective or rigid technique whereby one produces religious experience, *lectio divina* represents daily contact with God's word that occurs within a lifetime's engagement with the Living God. The principal aim of such engagement is to foster living prayer in faithful love. *Lectio divina* unfolds more than it proceeds, progresses and develops more than it advances. Dedicated practice engages the whole person—the intellect as well as the imagination, the will as well as the affect. It promises contact with God that is the normal fulfillment of prayer. *Lectio divina* is open to every person and not the exclusive property of a select few. Those who practice *lectio divina* reaffirm the belief that the proper place for the word of God is in the hands of the faithful.

Wouldn't Geppetto have been pleased if, instead of his firm response, "Pinocchio," that young man had looked into Jay Leno's TV camera and answered with conviction, "Jonah"?

NOTES

This chapter is reprinted with permission from *Chicago Studies* 39 (2000): 211–19.

1. "Spiritual Exercises," in *Ignatius of Loyola*, ed. George Ganns (Mahwah, NJ: Paulist, 1991), 122.

2. Quoted by Enzo Bianchi, *Pregare La Parola* (Milan: Piero Gribaudi Editore, 1996), 106–7.

3. Quoted by Mario Masini, *La Lectio Divina* (Milan: Edizioni San Paolo, 1996), 418.

4. Carlo Maria Martini, *Ritrovare Se Stessi* (Casale Monferrato: Piemme, 1996), 60–61.

5. Quoted by Bianchi, *Pregare La Parole*, 110.

6. Quoted by Masini, *La Lectio Divina*, 430.

7. Carlo Maria Martini, "Lectio Divina e pastorale," in *Ascolto della Parola e Preghiera: La Lectio Divina* (Vatican City: Libreria Editrice Vaticana, 1987), 217.

8. Ibid.

14

COMING TO KNOW JESUS THROUGH CONTEMPLATION OF THE GOSPELS

William A. Barry, SJ

I f you are experiencing the desire to know Jesus more intimately you can begin with some contemplation of the Gospels. Contemplation, as Ignatius means it, is a rather simple way of using the Gospels for prayer. You begin each period of prayer by expressing your desire to know Jesus more intimately in order to love him more deeply and follow him more closely. Then you read a passage of the Gospels and let it stimulate your imagination in the way a good novel can.

People have different kinds of imaginations. Some are able to make something like a movie of each scene. They watch and listen as the scene unfolds in their imagination. I do not have that kind of imagination. I don't see anything, for the most part. My imagination is not pictorial; I seem to intuit the story or feel it. I was helped in understanding and trusting my imagination by realizing that I have visceral reactions to stories—I wince when I hear of someone hitting his finger with a hammer, and I weep when I hear people's stories of pain and loss. Each of us needs to be content with and trust the imagination we have. In contemplating the Gospel stories, don't be afraid to let your imagination go. The Gospels are stories written to engage our imaginations, hearts, and minds so that we will come to know, love, and follow Jesus. They are meant to elicit reactions and, ultimately, a faith that shows itself in action. They are not biographies or historical documents or theological discourses.

As you begin to contemplate the Gospels with the hope of getting to know and love Jesus more, it is important to remember that Jesus of Nazareth was a historical human being who was born in a small territory in Palestine controlled by the Roman Empire. It is difficult for many Christians to take seriously that Jesus was a real human being because of the training and teaching they have had. They can say that Jesus was fully human, but the emphasis of most catechetical training and preaching has been on his divinity. And, to be truthful, many Christians think that calling Jesus divine means that he knew everything, including the future; that he always knew what others were thinking, because he could read minds; and that he could do anything he wanted to do, because he was God. In reality, such a view of Jesus of Nazareth does not take his humanity seriously; many Christians consider Jesus's humanness only when reflecting on his horrible suffering at the crucifixion.

In contemplating the Gospels, take this advice to heart. Be sure to take Jesus's humanity seriously even as you reflect on his divine attributes. God took humanity seriously enough to become one of us, and we do God no service if we downplay what God has done in becoming human. When we use our imagination in the contemplative way Ignatius suggests, we trust that God's Spirit will use it to reveal something important for us about Jesus so that we will love him and want to follow him. The only way that we can get to know another person is through revelation; the other must reveal him- or herself to us. In contemplating the Gospels, we are asking Jesus to reveal himself to us.

Getting to know Jesus can be discomfiting, to say the least. Mark's Gospel (10:17–22) gives us an example of how disconcerted a person can become. A young man runs up to Jesus and asks, "Good Teacher, what must I do to inherit eternal life?"

> Jesus, looking at him, loved him and said, "You lack one thing; go, sell what you own, and give the money to the poor, and you will have treasure in heaven; then come, follow me." When he heard this, he was shocked and went away grieving, for he had many possessions. (10:21–22)

Because of this man's addiction to his possessions, he could not follow through on his desire to do more. Notice that he goes away grieving: he knows that he is losing something precious. How do you feel as you contemplate this scene?

You may occasionally find yourself feeling something like what this rich man felt. You, too, may want to follow Jesus completely but feel that something is standing in the way. You know that a total commitment to Jesus means sacrificing something in your life that you believe you cannot do without. What are you to do? After I gave a talk on prayer, a professor engaged me in this dialogue:

"I want a closer relationship with God, but I know that if I do get close to God, I will have to do something I do not want to do."

"Why don't you tell God that you don't want to do it?"

"Can I do that?"

"We are talking about a friendship here. You can tell God anything in your heart and then see how God responds."

That's the advice I would give you, too. Anything that comes up in these contemplations is grist for the mill of your relationship with Jesus. Remember that friendship develops through mutual transparency.

Does Jesus love the rich man any less when he goes away? Does he love the professor any less because he's stuck? If you have gotten to know Jesus, you will have an answer, I'm sure. For my part, I do not believe that Jesus loved the rich man any less, but I do believe that Jesus was disappointed. I suspect, however, that his disappointment stemmed from the fact that the man would not continue the dialogue but walked away. If he had stayed with Jesus, he might have been able to say, "I cannot give up my wealth, but I wish that I could. Help me." That would have continued the conversation, and the friendship would have grown.

NOTES

This chapter is reprinted with permission from *A Friendship Like No Other: Experiencing God's Amazing Embrace* (Chicago: Loyola, 2008), 54–57.

FURTHER READING ON ENCOUNTERING JESUS IN THE SCRIPTURES

Barry, William A. *Who Do You Say I Am: Meeting the Historical Jesus in Prayer*. Notre Dame, IN: Ave Maria Press, 1996.

Borg, Marcus, and N. T. Wright. *The Meaning of Jesus: Two Visions*. San Francisco: Harper, 1998.

Brown, Raymond E. *Christ in the Gospels of the Liturgical Year*. Collegeville, MN: Liturgical Press, 2008.

Burkett, Delbert, ed. *The Blackwell Companion to Jesus*. Blackwell Companions to Religion. Oxford, UK: Wiley-Blackwell, 2011.

Charlesworth, James H. *The Historical Jesus: An Essential Guide*. Nashville: Abingdon, 2008.

Gowler, David B. *What Are They Saying about the Historical Jesus*. New York: Paulist, 2007.

Harrington, Daniel J. *Historical Dictionary of Jesus*. Historical Dictionaries of Religions, Philosophies, and Movements 102. Lanham, MD: Scarecrow, 2010.

————. *Jesus: A Historical Portrait*. Cincinnati: St. Anthony Messenger Press, 2007.

Hurtado, Larry W. *How on Earth Did Jesus Become a God? Historical Questions about the Earliest Devotion to Jesus*. Grand Rapids: Eerdmans, 2005.

Levine, Amy-Jill. *The Misunderstood Jew: The Church and the Scandal of the Jewish Jesus.* San Francisco: HarperSanFrancisco, 2006.

———. ed. *The Historical Jesus in Context.* Princeton: Princeton University Press, 2006.

Lohfink, Gerhard. *Jesus of Nazareth: What He Wanted, Who He Was.* Collegeville, MN: Liturgical Press, 2012.

Magness, Jodi. *Stone and Dung, Oil and Spit: Jewish Daily Life in the Time of Jesus.* Grand Rapids: Eerdmans, 2011.

Meier, John P. *A Marginal Jew.* 4 vols. New York: Doubleday, 1991, 1994, 2001, 2009.

Ratzinger, Joseph (Pope Benedict XVI). *Jesus of Nazareth: From the Baptism to the Transfiguration.* New York: Doubleday, 2007.

———. *Jesus of Nazareth. Part 2, Holy Week: From the Entrance into Jerusalem to the Resurrection.* San Francisco: Ignatius, 2011.

Schweitzer, Albert. *The Quest of the Historical Jesus: First Complete Edition.* Ed. John Bowden. Minneapolis: Fortress, 2001.

Wright, N. T. *Jesus and the Victory of God.* Minneapolis: Fortress, 2003.

———. *Surprised by Hope: Rethinking Heaven, the Resurrection, and the Mission of the Church.* New York: HarperOne, 2008.

INDEX

actio, 93, 94–98

Acts of the Apostles, 50, 52

Acts of Pilate, 86

Ambrose, 84

Anxious about Empire (Avram, ed.), 38–39

apocryphal Gospels, 80–88

apokryphos, 80

Arabic Infancy Gospel, 85

art, Roman, 47

Ascension of Isaiah, 86

Augustus, Caesar, 36. *See also* Roman Empire

autoasphaleia ("truth itself"), 22

autobasileia ("the kingdom itself"), 22, 23

autodikaiosyne ("justice itself"), 22

autosophia ("wisdom itself"), 22

Avram, Wesley, 38–39

belief, 14, 18–19

Benedict, Saint, 90

Bible, 60–65; approved books (canon), 7; ignorance of, 89–90. *See also specific books*

Bible, the Jews and the Death of Jesus, The: A Collection of Catholic Documents (U.S. Conference of Catholic Bishops Committee for Ecumenical Affairs), 60–61

Bill of Rights, 30–31

Blaire, Stephen E., 60–61

Brazos Press, 38–39

Brown, Dan, 5, 7, 83

Brueggemann, Walter, 40

Bultmann, Rudolf, 1

Bush, George W., 38–39

C21 Resources, 2

Caesar: Jesus and Paul vs., 36–45; as "Savior," 37

Caesar, Julius, 36. *See also* Roman Empire

Caiaphas, 63–64

Canaanite woman, 50

Catholics, 89–90

Christian character and conduct, 29–31

Christian Jews, 41
Christian piety, early, 80–88
Christians, Jewish, 83–84
Church: approved books
(canon), 7; divorce of
Jesus from Judaism by,
53–59; early, 46–52;
women in, 46–52
Clement of Alexandria, 83–84
Colossians, Letter to, 52, 71
Constitution on Divine
Revelation (*Dei
verbum*), 2
contemplation, 100–103
Crossan, John Dominic, 21, 37,
42, 43–44
crucifixion: as a story of
hope, 72; terror of,
66–72
culture, material, 46–47

Da Vinci Code, The (Brown),
5, 7, 46, 52, 83
Declaration of Independence,
30–31
deicide, 65
deliberatio, 93, 96–97
discretio, 93, 96–97
Dunn, James D. G., 20
Dwyer, Timothy, 77–78

early Christian piety,
80–88
early Church, 46–52
Elliott, Neil, 41
empty tomb story, 73–79

Ephesians, Letter to, 71
epiclesis, 94, 96
Epiphanius, 83–84
Epistle of Barnabas, 86
Esquivel, Julia, 72
Esther (Queen), 49
ethics, 29–31
euangelion, 81
Eucharist, 94
Eusebius, 83–84, 86
Exodus, Book of, 49
exorcisms, 42

faith, 14, 18–19
Fiorenza, Elisabeth Schüssler,
39
First Corinthians, 21–22, 42,
51, 81
First Thessalonians, 81
free choice, 70–71
fringes (*tzitzit*), 56–57

Galatians, Letter to, 14–15, 62,
67, 81
Gandalf, 79
Gandhi, 24
gendered space, 49–50
Gerasa, 58
German Protestants, 1, 11
Gibson, Mel, 5
Gnostic Gospels, 85
Gnostics, 85
God: heart of, 89–99. *See also*
kingdom of God
Golden Rule, 24, 29
gospel (term), 81

Gospel according to the Apostles, 84
Gospel of Bartholomew, 85
Gospel of Gamaliel, 86
Gospel of Judas, 83
Gospel of Mary, 7, 85
Gospel of Nicodemus, 86
Gospel of Peter, 7, 80, 86–87
Gospel of Philip, 7, 80, 85
Gospel of Pseudo-Matthew, 85
Gospel of the Ebionites, 84
Gospel of the Hebrews, 84
Gospel of the Nazareans, 84
Gospel of the Twelve, 84
Gospel of Thomas, 7, 82, 85
Gospel of Truth, 85
Gospels: apocryphal, 80–88;
    as biographies of Jesus,
    1; contemplation of,
    100–103; development
    of, 8–9; Gnostic, 85;
    infancy, 85–86; on
    Jesus's identity, 6, 14–15;
    Jewish-Christian
    Gospels, 83–84; lost, 84;
    material that goes back
    to Jesus, 9; meaning of,
    62; noncanonical, 7;
    passion, 85–86; Synoptic,
    7, 63. *See also specific
    authors; books by name*
Guigo II, 92–93
Gwyther, Anthony, 39–40

heart, 89–99
Hebrews, Letter to, 19

Herculaneum, 46–47
Hillel, 63
historian's Jesus, 10–11
historical Jesus, 10–11, 43, 55;
    quest for, 1, 11
historical religions, 54–55
history, social, 47–49
Holy Spirit, 13–19
hope, 72
Horsley, Richard A., 37–38,
    40, 41–42, 43
Howard-Brook, Wes, 39–40

Ignatius of Loyola, 91
*In Search of Paul: How Jesus'
    Apostle Opposed Rome's
    Empire with God's
    Kingdom* (Crossan
    and Reed), 37
infancy Gospels, 85–86
Isaiah, Book of, 17, 67–68
Isaiah (person), 55, 86

James (apostle), 76, 84
Jerome, 83–84, 90, 93–94
Jesus. *See* Jesus of Nazareth
Jesus (ben Hananiah), 42–43
Jesus: A Marginal Jew (Meier),
    20
Jesus, historical, 10–11, 43, 55;
    quest for, 1, 11
Jesus and the Victory of God
    (Wright), 20
Jesus of Nazareth: as *auto-
    asphaleia*, 22; as
    autobasileia, 22, 23;

as *autodikaiosyne*, 22;
as *autosophia*, 22; birth
of, 13, 14, 16; burial of,
77; as conceived by
Holy Spirit, born of
Virgin Mary, 14–19;
crucifixion of, 42–43,
66–72; Davidic descent,
16; death of, 8, 61, 67–68;
divorce from Judaism,
53–59; empty tomb of,
73–79; execution of, 10;
fact vs. fiction, 5–12; as
forgiving victim, 71–72;
getting to know,
100–103; historian's,
10–11; as historical
human being, 101;
identity of, 1, 5–12,
17–18; infancy narra-
tives, 15–17; as Jewish, 1,
7, 53–54, 56, 57–59; as
King of the Jews, 64;
and kingdom of God,
20–23, 43–44; legendary,
80–88; major themes in
his teaching, 10; mate-
rial in the Gospels that
goes back to, 9; as
Messiah, 5, 6; ministry,
9–10; miracles of, 32–35;
as obedient son, 71;
parables, 55; passion of,
60–65, 86; prohibition of
taking oaths, 9; public
career, 9–10;

resurrection of, 72, 84;
vs. Roman Empire,
36–45; sacrifice for
others, 67–68; Sermon
on the Mount, 24–31;
Sermon on the Plain, 25;
as Son of God, 15, 26; as
son of Joseph, 17–18;
sources about, 6–8;
suffering, 69–70
Jesus Remembered (Dunn), 20
Jewish Antiquities
(Josephus), 8
Jewish-Christian Gospels,
83–84
Jewish Christians, 83–84
Jewish Law, 27
Jews, 54, 58–59, 60–65;
Christian Jews, 41
John (apostle), 76
John, Gospel of, 7, 13, 17–18;
on the crucifixion,
67, 69, 70, 71; on
identification of Jesus,
17–18; on Jesus and the
kingdom of God, 22;
and Jesus's family, 17–18;
on Jesus's identity, 6, 7,
79; view of Pilate, 63–64
John of Patmos, 39–40
John Paul II, 60–61
John the Baptist, 5–6, 9
Joseph, Saint, 17–18
Joseph of Arimathea, 77
Josephus, Flavius, 8
Judaism, 59, 62–63

Judas Iscariot, 76, 83
Judith (person), 49
justice, 22, 40–41
Justin Martyr, 86

Kahl, Brigitte, 39
King, Martin Luther, 24
kingdom of God: Jesus and,
    20–23, 43–44; Jesus as
    autobasileia, 22

Last Supper, 84
lectio, 93, 94–95
lectio divina, 90, 91–93, 98;
    practice of, 93–94; steps
    of, 92, 94–98
lectiones sanctas, 90
legendary Jesus, 80–88
Legion, 41–42, 58
Leno, Jay, 89, 90
"Letter on the Contemplative
    Life" (*Scala Claustralium*)
    (Guigo II), 92–93
Leviticus, Book of, 57, 67
Logos (Word of God), 17–18
Lord of the Rings, The
    (Tolkien), 79
Lord's Prayer, 10, 24, 26,
    27, 43
lost Gospels, 84
Luke, Gospel of: Christmas
    passage, 37; on the
    crucifixion, 63, 64, 71;
    infancy narrative, 15–17;
    on Jesus and the king-
    dom of God, 21, 22; on

Jesus's identity, 6, 7, 79;
    Sermon on the Plain, 25

M, 25
Mark, Gospel of: and
    apocryphal Gospels, 81,
    87; on the
    crucifixion, 66, 67–68,
    69, 71, 78; development
    of, 8; divorce of Jesus
    from Judaism, 57–58;
    Easter revelation, 79; on
    the empty tomb, 73–79;
    on Jesus and Paul vs.
    the Roman Empire,
    41–42, 43; on Jesus and
    the kingdom of God, 21;
    on Jesus's identity, 1, 6,
    15, 102; on miracles of
    Jesus, 34; *The Motif of
    Wonder in the Gospel of
    Mark*, 77–78; on the
    resurrection, 78; women
    in, 50, 77
Mary, 13–19
Mary Magdalene, 46, 50, 52,
    70
Mary mother of John Mark,
    52
material culture, 46–47
Matthew, Gospel of: and
    apocryphal Gospels, 84,
    87; great speeches by
    Jesus, 26; infancy
    narrative, 15–17; on
    Jesus and the kingdom

of God, 21, 22; on Jesus's identity, 6, 7, 9; Sermon on the Mount, 24–31; view of Pilate, 63–64; women in, 50

meditatio, 93, 95–96, 97

Meier, John P., 20

messiahship, 5

miracle workers, 33

miracles, 32–35

Miriam, 49

Motif of Wonder in the Gospel of Mark, The (Dwyer), 77–78

Mount Vesuvius, 46–47

mummy portraits, 47

New Testament: fundamental questions, 1; interpretation of, 61; women in, 49–50. *See also specific books*

New Testament Abstracts, 2–3

Nicodemus, 86

Numbers, Book of, 56

Nympha, 52

Octavius, 36

Old Testament, 34, 54. *See also specific books*

oratio, 93, 96–97

Origen, 83–84

Orthodox Jews, 56

parables, 55

parousia, 37

passion, the, 60–65, 86

passion Gospels, 85–86

Passion of the Christ, The (Gibson), 5

passion plays, 62

Paul: on the crucifixion, 67; on the gospel, 40, 81; on Jesus and the kingdom of God, 21–22; on Jesus's identity, 14–15; as a Jew, 44; vs. Roman Empire, 36–45

Paul and Empire (Horsley, ed.), 37–38, 40, 41

Paul and Politics Group (Society of Biblical Literature, SBL), 37–38

Pax Romana, 37

peace, 37

peacemaking, 38

Peter, 5, 50, 72, 76

Pharisees, 27, 57, 62–63

Phoebe, 52

piety, early Christian, 80–88

pigs, 57–58

Pilate, Pontius, 10, 63–65

Pompeii, 46–47

prayer, 93, 97–98

Protestants, German, 1, 11

Protevangelium of James, 80, 85

Psalms, Book of, 13

Q, 25

Reed, Jonathan L., 37, 43–44
Reflections, 38–39
Republican Party, 38–39
resurrection, 72, 78, 84
Revelation, Book of, 39–40
revelation, divine, 74
Roman Catechism, 61–62
Roman Empire: art of, 47;
    Jesus and Paul vs.,
    36–45; as normalcy of
    civilization, 44; *Paul and
    Empire*, 37–38, 40, 41;
    social history of, 48;
    Unveiling Empire,
    39–40; women in,
    51–52
Romans, Letter to: on the
    crucifixion, 67–68; on
    divorce of Jesus from
    Judaism, 53; on the
    gospel, 81; and taxes, 41;
    on women in the early
    Church, 50, 52
Rome. *See* Roman Empire
"The Roots of Anti-Judaism
    in the Christian Milieu"
    (John Paul II), 60–61
Rule of Saint Benedict, 90

sacra pagina, 93–94
sacrifice, 68–69
scandal of particularity, 54
Schweitzer, Albert, 1, 21, 29
Second Corinthians, 67, 81
Second Quest of Historical
    Jesus, 1

Second Vatican Council, 6,
    65, 90
Serapion, 86
Sermon on the Mount,
    24–31; on Christian
    character and conduct,
    29–31; genre, 28–29; as
    Jewish wisdom instruc-
    tion, 28–29; major sec-
    tions, 27–28; origin,
    context, and content,
    25–26; theological
    significance of,
    28–29
Sermon on the Plain, 25
social history, 47–49
Society of Biblical Literature
    (SBL), 37–38
Son of God. *See* Jesus of
    Nazareth
Spiritual Exercises (Ignatius
    of Loyola), 91
Stassen, Glen, 38
storytelling, 66–72
suffering, 69–70
Suffering Servant, 67–68
swine, 57–58
Synoptic Gospels, 7, 63, 87
Syro-Phoenician or
    Canaanite woman, 50

Tabitha/Dorcas, 50
Taussig, Hal, 39
taxes, 41
theological imaginations,
    82–83

orical

., 79
w (Leno), 89
, 85
(fringes), 56–57

Union Theological Seminary,
39
United States, 44
Unveiling Empire (Howard-
Brook and Gwyther),
39–40
U.S. Conference of Catholic
Bishops, 60

Vatican II, 2, 60, 65, 90
Virgin Mary, 13–19

widows, 50
wisdom, 22
women: appropriation of
Christian story, 68–72;
in early Church, 46–52;
and the empty tomb,
77; in New Testament,
49–50; in public life,
51–52; voices of, 51;
widows, 50. *See also
specific women
by name*
wonder, 77–78
Word of God, 17–18
Wright, N. T., 20, 37, 40, 42

Yom Kippur (Day of
Atonement), 67